Forgotten Soldiers

Fred Gaffen

Theytus Books Ltd.
Penticton, B.C.

Canadian Cataloguing in Publication Data

Gaffen, Fred.
    FORGOTTEN SOLDIERS

    ISBN 0-919441-10-6

    1. World War, 1939-1945—Participation, Indian.
    2. World War, 1914-1918—Participation, Indian.
    3. Veterans—Canada.
    4. Indians of North America—Canada. I. Title.

D810.I5G33   1984   940.54'04   C84-091374-5

Front Cover Art: Fred Stelkia
Cover design: Beyond Graphics
Typsetting by: Theytus Books

Printed and bound in Canada

Dedication

For Canada's Native Peoples who served in both World Wars.

A Forgotten Soldier

A symbolic representation of the book's purpose:
the rescue of the native veteran from oblivion in the public consciousness.
Fred Stelkia depicts two mythical outriders coming to the rescue of a wounded Indian soldier.

CONTENTS

APPENDICES

MAPS

Forewords

Opening Statements by Buffy Sainte Marie and E.A. "Smokey" Smith

I hate war! I hate the idea of war. I don't even like thinking about war; but I live in the same world you do, so I must think about it, hoping to avoid the real thing. I don't like fighting, conflict, anger, any of it.

Did you ever notice that as the politicians are getting us ready for war we are presented with movies, marching bands, art exhibits, stories of heroism and fireworks, all to psych us up to want to participate? We're all saps to go for it. I agree that decorations and uniforms and Sousa marches can be dazzling, but I'm the one who wrote "The Universal Soldier" and "Moratorium" and other stuff deglamorizing war, and it's clear by now that I'm scared to death of nuclear possibilities, famine, death, etc; so why am I writing a foreword to this book?

Because some real human stories of our Indian people are told here, and those people happen to be soldiers, or the loved ones of soldiers.

I know veterans of Vietnam. They're my relatives and my friends, and I love them. They told me about the excitement of getting out of their home towns and how they anticipated a trip overseas; about the patriotism in their hearts as they signed up; about their disillusionment with the realities of all they went through over there, and my heart spreads out on the ground for them.

I've sat beside my uncles around a table or a fire or drum and heard about the Second World War and Korea—some of it was funny and—some of it tragic.

The whole point is this: I don't like wars any better for my relatives' stories, but I do like my relatives. And whenever I see the flag carried into the circle by a veteran, behind our eagle staff Indian flag, I'm proud of our people. And as for those of our people who were soldiers and remembered here, I wish they had all come back home.

"STAR SOLDIER"

A love song to her sweetheart or husband who is leaving. It could be 1890 or 1990. Her soldier might carry a lance, or a "coup-stick"* or a briefcase full of legal documents, or simply an Eagle Feather and Medicine Bundle; his enemy is the greed in the human heart, and the prize is a living sacred peace that comes from within the culture, envelops and neutralizes the spiritual enemy, and returns to the circle of loved ones.

You hear my heart is calling, calling,
Calls you, calls you,
Come to the one who needs you *Sice* (my relative)
Oh, Ohh, now it's time to part and
Star soldier, I will wait for you
Ke Sakihetin (I love you) star soldier Oh
So go your way then come and bring me
All it is you have to give me
All you keep in your heart my dear
All you keep in your heart, *Sice*.

*A stick used by Plains' warriors to demonstrate their bravery against the enemy. For example, a warrior might charge the enemy alone armed only with this stick and quickly tap a chief in order to demonstrate his bravery.

I am happy to contribute a foreword to this work. It makes available new information about this country's native peoples in both World Wars. As well as describing their accomplishments on the battlefield, the book takes the home front into consideration. Amidst the many pressures of daily living, we often forget or ignore contributions and sacrifices made in the past. Canada's native people have made great personal sacrifices in both World Wars on this nation's behalf. Let us take pride in their accomplishments and strive to ensure that they are not forgotten.

Having fought alongside many Indians in the Second World War, with so many displaying coolness and courage under fire, I was proud to serve with them. I was pleased at long last their service to Canada is recognized in this book, and am sure other veterans will gain the same pleasure in reading it.

I hope that the accounts of courage and sacrifice contained herein will help make current and future generations of native youth aware of their predecessors' contributions and inspire them to meet the problems and challenges of the present and future.

E.A. "Smokey" Smith, VC, CD

Preface

After watching television items about Canada's aboriginal peoples and the Constitution, I asked myself why don't they ever speak of their service in either of the World Wars. Was it not worthy of mention? My curiosity was aroused. There must be a book somewhere on this subject, I thought. Several exhaustive searches revealed that such a book had never been written.

To most North Americans the subject of the Indian and his military service in both World Wars has been of marginal interest. Johnny Cash in one of his best selling records, the *Ballad of Ira Hayes,* publicized the case of one Indian. It is hoped this study will shed light on others and will give Canadian Indians who fought and were killed some recognition.

Perhaps their military service has been ignored because they never comprised more than a small percentage of the total Canadian forces employed. As well, they were scattered among various units, mostly in the army. Several joined the navy and merchant marine, and some the air force.

Life in the armed forces for the native soldier, like any other, did not consist of continuously fighting the enemy. Much of the time was spent training, drilling and doing various monotonous chores. Some who wished to go overseas never went but spent the war in Canada performing guard duty. Several deserted. From casualty lists, it is apparent that the First World War caused greater loss of life and injuries than the Second.

On going through the text, the reader will find that many Indian surnames are the same. This is largely the result of a common ancestor, for example, Joseph Brant, the great leader of the Six Nations who fought on the British side in the war of the American Revolution. In the text, I have only identified immediate family relationships such as a brother or father among those killed. If an individual was known as an Indian or Metis or (Inuk) Eskimo, he has been so identified.

I have had to narrow my selection of individuals mainly to those who were decorated for bravery, sacrificed their lives or achieved recognition. A random selection of those killed in the major actions can be found in the main text. As some relatives are unaware of the theatre or battle or even precise date of death of a loved one, I have included basic information about each fatality in the appendices. The date of death, for example, June 6, 1944 (D Day) will give some indication as to the particular battle and theatre.

This account is not, of course, intended to glorify war. The long list of those who gave their lives bears testimony to war's consequences. Nevertheless, in the midst of battle, qualities such as bravery and self-sacrifice make their appearance and it is these qualities that are recognized.

I have included both treaty and non-treaty Indians as well as those having only some native blood. Although some names are definitely Indian—for example, Second World War recruits with surnames such as Rattlesnake, Yellowbank, Whitecloud, Redsky, Manywounds—most names are no different from those of the rest of the population.

Canada's native people suffered their share of casualties in both World Wars. In every major Canadian land battle they were in the front line. Their contribution must never be forgotten.

My deepest regret in preparing this manuscript was the lack of funds that prevented my securing better photos or travelling in order to meet and interview native veterans and their families. A shortage of good documentary records also proved to be a severe handicap. During the course of my research I have come across both prejudice and good will. If this account helps in some way to foster greater understanding, it will have been worth the sacrifice of leisure time that could have been more enjoyably spent with my wife and our young family. My appreciation to William Constable who prepared maps 1 and 5, and to the Directorate of History for permission to use numbers 2, 3 and 4. I am indebted to Frank McGuire for editorial assistance. My sincere thanks to all who helped or contributed.

Fred Gaffen

A Retrospect

Few Indian veterans of the First World War are still alive. Even fewer remain who fought overseas. For some, memories and recollections of events have faded with the passage of time. The following is a brief personal account supplied to me by Alfred J. Cook, born July 9, 1898, on the former St. Peters Reserve near Selkirk and now a member of the Bloodvein Band in Manitoba. It gives me some insight as to what it felt like to be a Canadian infantryman on the Western Front. Photos more visibly reveal what had to be endured.

I enlisted in Brandon, January 1, 1917, and joined the 249th Battalion stationed at Regina. We left Regina on the 12th of May for Halifax and were about six days on the train. We boarded the troopship *Olympic* and were on it about 24 hours when our unit was taken off and moved to a military camp at Aldershot, Nova Scotia. On June 3, 1917, we were moved to Camp Valcartier for training, where we remained until October. During the fall and winter, we were in Quebec City. In March of 1918, we arrived in England and our battalion was absorbed into the 15th Reserve Battalion. In June, I was asked what outfit I wanted, so I chose 'the good old fighting 5th'. I joined that battalion at Arras in France. In early August 1918 they took us down to Amiens, the day before the big offensive....

I never drank any intoxicating alcohol all the time I was in the army but this morning I was coaxed to take some rum. I was told I would need it. I took a big drink and it almost choked me. In Indian 'Eskotawaowitch' means fire water. I'll say it was fire water. I was really set on fire. I was going to clean up the whole German Army. For-

tunately, I was kept down.

Suddenly, all hell opened up. This old world was just trembling. We couldn't hear a thing so we used signs. Minutes after the barrage lifted we were given the signal to advance. When we got to the enemy's front line, it was a terrible sight. There were bodies all over the place blown to pieces, heads, legs, arms, guts.

About two o'clock in the afternoon I went down into the dugout sat down and fell asleep. I don't know how long I slept. When I awoke there was a young lad next to me I didn't know, so I called him 'Scottie'. There wasn't a sign of any of my comrades. I climbed out of the trench onto the parapet and I saw enemy helmets approaching. I said to my friend: 'We must have taken them prisoners.' As soon as the Germans saw us, they started hollering and we realized they weren't prisoners. There must have been a 100 of them. We began running. They started shooting at us and this is God's truth, bullets were flying around us like rain. I could hear bullets whiz by my ears. Shells began exploding around us but we managed to reach our comrades unhurt.

The advance continued until the enemy reached the 1916 trenches where they stopped us for a few weeks. We broke through the German lines and advanced to Cambrai...We took Cambrai but it sure cost us a lot of our boys. From there we advanced driving the enemy back. It was just a rout in Belgium. On November 11, 1918, we were billetted in a building with nice armchairs and chesterfields. This was paradise.... Then we were on our way into Germany. I marched for three days and took sick with flu. I was sent back to the base hospital and left France on January 2, 1919.

While Alfred Cook was able to adapt, other Indians found the transition more difficult. To understand some of the problems faced by Canadian Indians who served, especially in the First World War, it is necessary to have some insight into their history and culture with respect to warfare. Before the white man came, Indians, especially those in eastern Canada, viewed the death of an individual as a vital loss to the social group. Thus, heavy casualties were to be avoided. The tactics of the Indians included stealth and concealment. Their main weapons were bows and arrows, spears, clubs and, to a lesser extent, javelins. Wooden shields and breastplates were relatively effective against the arrow.

When Samuel de Champlain joined a Huron-Algonquin war party in 1609 and killed two Iroquois with the shot from his harquebus, a new era began for the Indians. No longer was it possible for them to advance in mass formation with shields raised. The only protection from the firearms and the greater killing power of the white man was in dispersion, sniping and ambush. This style of fighting was adopted by the French who became as skillful as the Indians in this type of war, termed *la petite guerre*. It was also copied by frontier units from the American colonies.

In North America during the 17th and 18th centuries, the European countries and their colonists sought to employ the native people as military auxiliaries. Prior to the British conquest of the New France, Indians had generally fought as allies of the French although the British also had Indian allies, notably among the Iroquois. In the last struggle between France and England in North America, Indians assisted both sides. Some Indian snipers were even present on September 13, 1759, at Quebec as allies of the French.

During the late 19th century in Canada, the British army and its style exerted a strong influence on Canada's military forces. The Indians, particularly those in remote areas, however, had little contact or training with the regular forces of Britain or Canada or with the militia. For many, ideas about and skills required in warfare remained rooted in their history and culture. Although familiar with firearms, many were not accustomed to the regimentation of the white soldier. For many who joined the Canadian Expeditionary Force in the First World War, and even some who served in the Canadian Army in the Se-

cond World War, the cultural shock was severe. They were expected to quickly adopt the white man's ways, including his military traditions and methods. For the Metis recruit, whose culture was unique yet closer to that of general Canadian society, the transition was not as difficult.

The Metis, the offspring of white (mainly French) and Indian parents, evolved as a distinct group, particularly on the prairies. The transfer to the Canadian government by the Hudson's Bay Company of its territory, from the Red River to the Rockies, created a crisis as the way of life of the Metis was threatened. Led by Louis Riel, they rose up in 1870 to defend what they considered their rights and helped bring about the entry of Manitoba into Confederation. Some Metis from this group moved west, many reestablishing themselves along the North Saskatchewan River. Commencing in March 1885, again under Louis Riel's leadership, they took up arms against the Canadian government to defend their rights and customs. The Canadian forces proved too strong. Riel was taken prisoner on May 15th and hanged for treason on November 16th.

The terrible plight of many Metis in remote areas came to public attention in the period between the World Wars, particularly the decade prior to the Second World War. The Great Depression, drought on the prairies and the ending of squatters' rights in Alberta, all combined to exacerbate their desperate situation. By organizing in Alberta and elsewhere the Metis attracted the attention of governments. Steps were taken to help such as improved health, education and welfare services and the establishment of Metis settlements. Great progress has been made and is continuing.

Prior to the 20th century the Inuit of the Northwest Territories had relatively little to do with white society. In Labrador, however, there was more contact with whites. This was a significant factor in the enlistment of Inuit from this region.

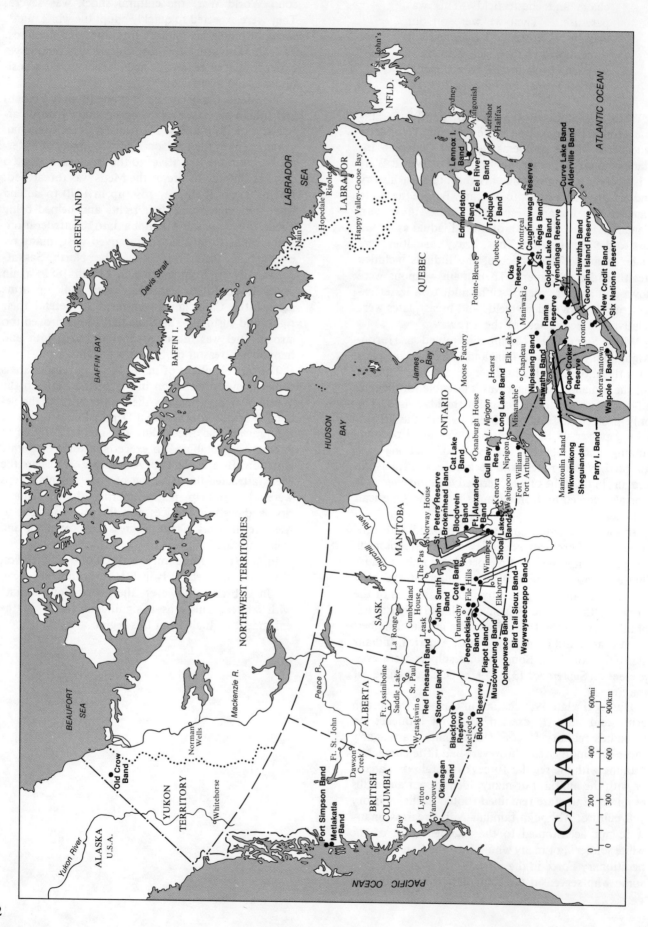

CANADA

ALASKA
U.S.A.

YUKON TERRITORY

NORTHWEST TERRITORIES

BRITISH COLUMBIA

ALBERTA

SASK.

MANITOBA

ONTARIO

QUEBEC

NFLD.

GREENLAND

BAFFIN I.

BAFFIN BAY

HUDSON BAY

James Bay

LABRADOR

LABRADOR SEA

Davis Strait

BEAUFORT SEA

PACIFIC OCEAN

ATLANTIC OCEAN

Yukon River
Mackenzie R.
Peace R.
Churchill River

Old Crow Band
Port Simpson Band
Metlakatla Band
Okanagan Band
Stoney Band
Blackfoot Reserve
Blood Reserve
Red Pheasant Band
John Smith Band
Punnichy Cote Band
Peepeekisis Band
Piapot Band
Muscowpetung Band
Ochapowace Band
Waywayseecappo Band
Bird Tail Sioux Band
St. Peters Reserve
Brokenhead Band
Ft. Alexander Band
Bloodvein Band
Cat Lake Band
Shoal Lake Band
Gull Bay Band
Long Lake Band
Nipissing Band
Hiawatha Band
Rama Reserve
Golden Lake Band
St. Regis Band
Caughnawaga Reserve
Tyendinaga Reserve
Oka Reserve
Edmundston Band
Tobique Band
Eel River Band
Lennox I. Band
Curve Lake Band
Alderville Band
Georgina Island Reserve
New Credit Band
Six Nations Reserve
Cape Croker Reserve
Walpole I. Band
Parry I. Band
Manitoulin Island
Wikwemikong
Sheguiandah

Whitehorse
Ft. St. John
Dawson Creek
Norman Wells
Ft. Assiniboine
Saddle Lake
St. Paul
Wetaskiwin
Macleod
La Ronge
Cumberland House
Leask
File Hills
Elkhorn
Norway House
The Pas
Winnipeg
Osnaburgh House
Moose Factory
Hearst
Chapleau
Elk Lake
Missanabie
Wabigoon
Nipigon
L. Nipigon
Kenora
Fort William
Port Arthur
Maniwaki
Pointe-Bleue
Quebec
Montreal
Toronto
Moraviantown
Lytton
Vancouver
Alert Bay
Nain
Hopedale
Rigolet
Happy Valley-Goose Bay
Sydney
Antigonish
Aldershot
Halifax
St. John's

0   200   400   600mi
0   300   600   900km

12

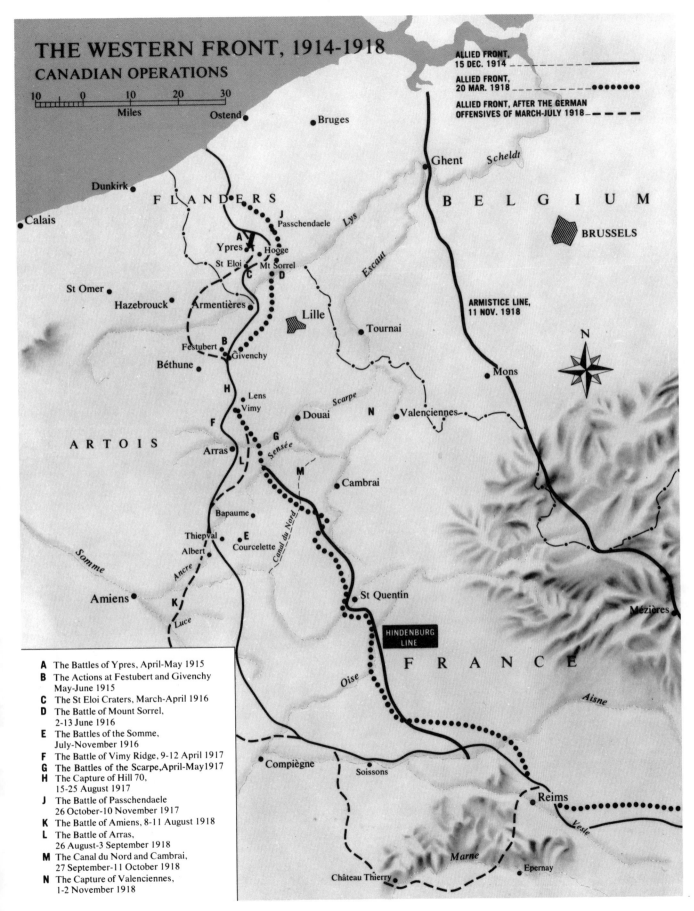

THE WESTERN FRONT, 1914-1918
CANADIAN OPERATIONS

10 0 10 20 30
Miles

ALLIED FRONT,
15 DEC. 1914 ————————

ALLIED FRONT,
20 MAR. 1918 ●●●●●●●●

ALLIED FRONT, AFTER THE GERMAN
OFFENSIVES OF MARCH-JULY 1918 — — —

Ostend

Bruges

Ghent *Scheldt*

Dunkirk

F L A N D E R S

B E L G I U M

Calais

Passchendaele *Lys*

J

A

Ypres Hooge

St Eloi Mt Sorrel

C   D

BRUSSELS

Escaut

St Omer

Hazebrouck

Armentières

Lille

Tournai

ARMISTICE LINE,
11 NOV. 1918

N

B

Festubert Givenchy

Béthune

Mons

H

Lens

Vimy *Scarpe*

Douai

N

Valenciennes

F

A R T O I S

Arras L *Sensée*

G

M

Cambrai

Bapaume

Canal du Nord

Thiepval E

Albert Courcelette

Somme

Ancre

Amiens K

Luce

St Quentin

HINDENBURG
LINE

F R A N C E

Oise

Mézières

Aisne

A The Battles of Ypres, April-May 1915
B The Actions at Festubert and Givenchy
   May-June 1915
C The St Eloi Craters, March-April 1916
D The Battle of Mount Sorrel,
   2-13 June 1916
E The Battles of the Somme,
   July-November 1916
F The Battle of Vimy Ridge, 9-12 April 1917
G The Battles of the Scarpe, April-May 1917
H The Capture of Hill 70,
   15-25 August 1917
J The Battle of Passchendaele
   26 October-10 November 1917
K The Battle of Amiens, 8-11 August 1918
L The Battle of Arras,
   26 August-3 September 1918
M The Canal du Nord and Cambrai,
   27 September-11 October 1918
N The Capture of Valenciennes,
   1-2 November 1918

Compiègne

Soissons

Reims

Vesle

Marne

Château Thierry

Epernay

PART I

THE FIRST WORLD WAR

Introduction

Although warfare was certainly not new to Canada's Indians or whites, the First World War was the first introduction on a large scale to military ser-

Lt. Cameron D. Brant, 4th Battalion   (Private Collection)

vice overseas and to weapons such as poison gas, the machine gun, the tank and the airplane as well as to close contact with those from different backgrounds. Skills such as scouting and marksmanship, however, were still prized. Indians did not wear distinctive uniforms but were dressed and equipped the same as other Canadian troops.

Much more than in the white community the warrior had prestige and status in traditional Indian society. For some Indians a motive for enlisting was the opportunity to assert their manhood. It may be of interest to some to note that some ceremonial roles which had previously been restricted to those braves with war experiences in North America were later conferred upon courageous Indian soldiers who fought overseas in either of the World Wars. In reading the accounts that earned native Canadians military decorations on the battlefields of both World Wars, it becomes apparent that the skills of the Indian hunter and warrior came to the fore.

For Indians who had been raised in the traditional way there was some unique problems of adjusting to army life, particularly in the relationship between officers and men. Traditionally, among Indians, there was not the same sharp distinction between a war chief and warriors as between commissioned officers and other ranks. A war chief was considered by warriors more of an equal. If a particular warrior did not like or agree with one war chief he was usually not constrained from moving to another or from leaving the war party. While it would be customary practice for a chief to offer a warrior entering his tepee food or refreshments, and to treat him as an equal, such familiarity did not normally exist between commissioned officers and other ranks of the Canadian Corps.

The Battles

Ypres

With the British declaration of war on Germany on August 4, 1914, Canada was automatically at war as well. The training of the future 1st Canadian Division began at Valcartier, Quebec and continued on a rain-soaked Salisbury Plain in England. In February 1915 the division, nearly 20,000 strong, crossed to France. One Canadian battalion, Princess Patricia's Canadian Light Infantry (PPCLI), was already fighting in the area of Ypres in Belgium.

In April 1915 the Canadians faced a major battle in the Ypres salient in Belgium, where they stood their ground in the face of a new weapon—poison gas. One of the first, if not the first Indian to die in the fighting was Private Angus LaForce, a Mohawk from Caughnawaga, Quebec, on April 22. Another Indian who fell in the same battle was Lieutenant Cameron

Storming Vimy Ridge. Disarmed prisoners can be seen in foreground (Public Archives of Canada)

D. Brant from the New Credit Band near Hagersville, Ontario, killed while leading a counter-attack on 23/24 April. Also in the Ypres salient, Private Angus Splicer of the PPCLI was killed on June 4, 1916. He had joined the unit as a reinforcement in August 1915. Prior to enlisting, Splicer, a member of the Caughnawaga Band, had been a law student (1912-15) at McGill University. In the same month a Fort William Indian in the 52nd Battalion, Private Augustus Belanger, won the Military Medal (MM). The citation reads:

> On June 5, 1916, this man carried important despatches...to front line companies crossing a mile and a half of open country under intensely heavy shell fire...Although buried in a trench by the debris from bursting shells, he continued his journey, twice coming under machine gun fire, and safely delivered the despatches...During the whole of the period of the 3rd to 14th June, his conduct in delivering messages was most conspicuous.[1]

Private Thomas Godchere, 102nd Battalion
(Public Archives of Canada)

16

The Battles of the Somme
July - November 1916

The remainder of the 1916 can be summed up in two ominous words—the Somme. The Allied offensive began on July 1, 1916, but the Canadian Corps was not committed to battle until September. An Ojibway from Nipigon, Ontario, Private Joseph De Laronde of the 52nd Battalion, earned his Military Medal there:

> For conspicuous gallantry while acting as a guide to stretcher bearer parties and in carrying wounded men back from the front line under very heavy artillery fire. He worked without rest for two days. An Indian by birth, he gave a splendid example of the courage and perseverance of his race.

Vimy Ridge
April 9-14, 1917

Vimy Ridge, in northern France, had been fortified by the Germans with well wired trenches, deep dugouts, inter-connecting tunnels and concrete strong points. It was an important pivot in the enemy's defences. There on Easter Monday, April 9, 1917, came the Allies' first successful major offensive on the Western Front. On that day the entire Canadian Corps of four divisions, under British Commander, Lieutenant General Sir Julian Byng, took the heights of Vimy which became a symbol of Canadian achievement.

An Ojibway, Private Thomas Godchere of the Long Lake Band, Longlac, Ontario, was awarded the Military Medal:

> For gallant and distinguished conduct in reconnoitring and scouting under heavy shell and rifle fire after the attack...on the 9th April 1917. This man has always shown great coolness and daring while out on scouting patrols.

Thomas Godchere was killed in action when he made his final patrol that day.

Hill 70
August 1917

Following the success at Vimy Ridge, Field Marshal Sir Douglas Haig resolved to strike again hoping to achieve a breakthrough in Flanders. As a diversion, the Canadian Corps was ordered to capture Hill 70, north of Arras. On August 15 the Canadians took the hill in a dashing assault and held it firmly against successive counter-attacks. Among those who fell that day was Private Robert Tobico of the Alderville Band, near Rice Lake, Ontario.

Passchendaele
October - November 1917

Although the offensive in Flanders met with little success, Haig persisted in his attacks. The autumn rains set in and turned the shelled landscape into a

Private Isaac Maracle   (Bernice Maracle)

morass. Between October 26 and November 20, the Canadians fought in the mud and succeeded in taking the ruins of Passchendaele village and ridge and an area of flooded swamp. After the offensive the Canadians left the Ypres salient, never to return. Their later battles were fought farther south, mainly on French soil.

Private Isaac Maracle, a non-treaty Mohawk from the Bay of Quinte, a member of the PPCLI, was killed during an attack on October 30, 1917. His friend

Passchendaele (Public Archives of Canada)

and neighbour, Private Reuben Sero, a fellow Mohawk in the PPCLI, was killed at the same time. Both men had gone overseas together with the 155th and had transferred in July 1917 to the PPCLI.

Private Enos Williams of Ohsweken (Brantford), Ontario, won the Military Medal:

> At Passchendaele November 6, 1917, this man assisted materially in the capture of an enemy machine gun which was immediately brought into action against the enemy. On two occasions his gun was buried and both times he promptly recovered it and kept it in action. Under heavy shelling he returned back over captured ground to bring up ammunition for the gun.

The Last Hundred Days

Striking out from Amiens late in August 1918, the Canadian Corps pierced the Drocourt-Queant Line, an extension of the Hindenburg Line, crossed the Canal du Nord and freed Cambrai, the hub of the German communications system on the Western Front. The Indians of the 52nd Battalion played a notable role in these operations. Sergeant Leo Bouchard, an Indian from Lake Nipigon, Ontario, in the 52nd won the Distinguished Conduct Medal (DCM). The citation reads:

> For conspicuous gallantry and devotion to duty. He has served with his battalion continuously for nearly three years. He has at all times shown marked personal courage, initiative and skill in handling his men, particularly during the heavy fighting of August

1918. On one occasion when his officer was killed, he assumed command, and though isolated from the rest of his company and in the midst of dense fog, he led his men through the enemy barrage to their objective.

A member of the Shoal Lake Band, Private David Kisek (also Kejick, the village on the north shore of Shoal Lake, Ontario, named in his honour) of the 52nd Battalion at 6 ft. 1 in. one of the taller men in his regiment, was awarded the DCM because:

> He displayed marked courage and intelligence during the attack on enemy positions at Tilloy on 1st October 1918. When his company was held up by heavy fire, he on his own initiative ran into the open, and, with his Lewis gun at the hip, fired four pans into the enemy machine guns. His fire was so effective that a party of the company on the right were able to advance and capture four machine guns together with about 70 prisoners....

In looking through official photos of the First and Second World Wars, I have often wondered about the people in the pictures. One First World War veteran, Joe Daniels, a Metis, was able to recall his photo being taken. It was during the Battle of Amiens, 8 August 1918. He had marched to this area at night in order to avoid enemy detection. Some readers may be familiar with the name of his eldest son, Stan, a former president of the Metis Association of Alberta.

The Corps broke the next German defensive line during the last week of October at the outskirts of

Private David Kisek (Public Archives)

Valenciennes, Private David Faithful of the Port Simpson Band, Port Simpson, British Columbia won the Military Medal.

> This scout in front of Valenciennes on November 1, 1918, rendered invaluable assistance to his company in the advance by going well forward and sniping and putting out of action several enemy riflemen and machine guns, who were troubling our men.
> When the final objectives had been reached a party of the enemy were seen attempting to prevent our consolidation. Although the enemy artillery fire was extremely heavy, Private Faithful climbed to the top of the chimney and dispersed the party by rifle fire.
> His great daring under extremely heavy fire and his skill and gallantry were of invaluable assistance to the success of the operation.

On November 10 the Canadians triumphantly entered Mons, the scene of the first engagement between British and German troops in 1914. Next morning, at eleven o'clock, hostilities ceased.

Outside the Corps

Not all of Canada's soldiers served in the Canadian Corps. Of 150,000 Canadians on the Western Front at the end of the war 40,000 were outside Currie's command and they, too, had a splendid record. Among them were the Canadian Cavalry Brigade, railway troops, tunnelling companies and forestry units. A significant number of Canada's Indians served as railway troops and in pioneer and forestry units. In all theatres, soldiers of native ancestry could be found. Some Indians from Canada also served as pioneers with British forces.

Enlistment Across Canada

At the time of the First World War, North American Indians were not unknown to the people in western Europe. Many had an incomplete somewhat romantic view of the Indian. Sources of information included Wild West shows, artifacts in museums and a variety of literature. Many Canadians also had similar misconceptions about the Indian. Many were unaware of the social and cultural changes that Indian people were undergoing. A particular aspect of Indian history that received wide publicity, and often became synonymous with the Indian in the minds of many, was the former practice of torturing captives and scalping victims. With this stereotyped association, the reaction of whites having no contact with Indians becomes more understandable.

Soon after the outbreak of war in August 1914 the question was raised as to the desirability of enlisting Indians. It was decided not to accept them on the grounds that "while British troops would be proud to be associated with their fellow subjects, yet Germans might refuse to extend to them the privileges of civilized warfare."[2] However, many had already enlisted and were to be sent overseas. A considerable number of militia units seem to have either been unaware of the prohibition or else ignored it.

Some 3,500 treaty Indians enlisted for active service out of a total Indian population of 100,000 according to the surviving records of the Department of Indian Affairs.[3] There were also enlistments of Indians not living on reserves. The Indians usually joined a local battalion but in many cases became scattered throughout the Canadian Expeditionary Force. Significant numbers were in the 107th and 114th Battalions. In Quebec, some of the English speaking Indians there joined non-Quebec based battalions such as the 114th Battalion. Two exceptional Indian members of the 22nd Battalion from Quebec were both scouts—Private Willie Cleary, a Montagnais Indian from Pointe-Bleue on Lac Saint-Jean, and Private Joseph Roussin, an Iroquois from the Oka Reserve. Both received the Military Medal for bravery at Hill 70 near Lens.[4]

It is feasible to assess Indian participation and activities only through the various records of the Departments of National Defence, Indian Affairs, and Veterans Affairs. For the First World War it was impossible to ascertain precise numbers of Indian enlistments. In official military records, all Canadian born were treated alike as "Canadian". The only question on the attestation form on this point read: "In what town, township or parish and in what country were you born?" Subsequent information sometimes does reveal if the individual was an Indian.

The first major attempt to recruit Indians was by William Hamilton Merritt, an honorary chief of the Six Nations (Ohsweken), a prominent member of the militia and wealthy mining engineer, who in late 1914 proposed the establishment of a Six Nations Battalion at Brantford, Ontario. He modified his offer in early 1915 offering to contribute $5,000 to equip two companies of Six Nations Indians as part of an all Indian battalion commanded by white officers. The Militia Council considered his offer "inconvenient" and a Council of the Chiefs decided not to act on the proposal.[6] In December of 1915, owing

to the need for more men, the Minister of Militia and Defence, Sir Sam Hughes, granted official permission for Indians to enlist, thus rescinding his previous policy.[7]

During much of the hostilities in North America over two centuries, the Six Nations often remained officially neutral. On an individual basis warriors frequently had supported whomever they wished.[8] After the outbreak of the First World War, the Council of the Six Nations at Ohsweken (Brantford), composed of traditional chiefs, did not accept Merritt's offer. Considering themselves a separate national entity, the Council wanted a formal request from the

Ojibways in the 52nd Battalion wait in line for a meal. (Canadian War Records)

Crown that recognized this status, a request which the Canadian government did not wish to give. This position of the Council as well as many other matters and considerations caused federal authorities to later support a democratically elected Council. Among those on the Ohsweken Reserve in the vanguard pushing for an elected council were returned soldiers.

Of all the Indians in Canada, Ontario Indians enlisted in the largest numbers. Most came from the Six Nations Reserve near Brantford, and the Tyendinaga Reserve near Desoronto on the Bay of Quinte. The record of the Mississauga Indians near Peterborough is also noteworthy. One of them, Lance Corporal Johnson Paudash of the Hiawatha Band, Keene, Ontario, a scout and sniper "accounted for over 42 Huns by sniping" by March 1918.[9] Some give his final total as 88.[10] His most significant scouting action had been to warn of an enemy counter-attack at Hill 70, which helped to earn him the Military Medal.

Among the Ojibways or Chippewas in Ontario, many of their most able members went to the front. Especially noteworthy was the high rate of enlistment of Ojibways from the Lakehead area and the Nipigon district. The majority of the Indian recruits from this region joined the 52nd (popularly known as the "Bull Moose" Battalion) and the 94th and 141st Battalions.

Indians who enlisted, particularly those from remote areas during the First World War, had to face a severe culture shock as they adapted to military life. For some, proper military dress and deportment were very foreign to their way of life. But once in the services and acclimatized, the Indians generally proved to be ones who complained the least.

Learning of the death by pneumonia of William Johnson from Curve Lake, Ontario, Sergeant J. Moore described him to the Indian Agent "as one of the most faithful of the battalion, never had a pass, never even asked for a day off, never complaining and a brave fearless soldier."[11]

The account of William Semia from the Cat Lake Band in northern Ontario as recounted to his Indian Agent offers some insight into the experiences of Indians from remote areas. When Semia enlisted, he did not understand English and had to be assisted by a fellow Ojibway member with basic training. Port Arthur with its railways, street cars and large steamers was entirely different from anything he had known previously. For some days after he joined, Private Semia was afraid of being lost in the city and would not leave the armoury without another soldier.

Like so many other soldiers, Semia made the transatlantic crossing on the troopship, *Olympic*. In France, Semia transferred to the 52nd Battalion. He described Passchendaele "as a pretty bad fight." A few days later he was seriously wounded. Following extensive hospital care in England, Semia returned to Port Arthur for additional convalescence. Upon being discharged, he made his way back to Sioux Lookout via the railway and then, like most others from remote areas in Canada, returned home by canoe and on foot. Semia was able to secure a job operating a small steam boat for the Hudson's Bay Company store at Osnaburgh House during the summer months. Would he enlist again? "Next war me join 1st Battalion, first contingent,"[12] he told the Indian Agent shortly after his return.

Indians from the three Maritime provinces also enlisted in considerable numbers. The reserves in Nova Scotia were sparsely populated yet, proportionately, enlistment was quite high. The Micmacs of Sydney sent every eligible man to the forces. On the other hand, little interest in the war was shown by some including the Tobique and Edmundston Bands from New Brunswick.[13] Indians from the Maritimes particularly distinguished themselves in the Battle of Amiens in August 1918.

The contribution of the Indians from Lennox Island, Prince Edward Island, was particularly noteworthy. Lieutenant Ernest A. Strong of the 26th Battalion, while convalescing in hospital in England, described their contribution:

"Lennox Island need never be ashamed but be very proud of the work all their boys are doing and have done at the front. Let 'AMIENS' be inscribed on their records as a sacred city in France that their gallant boys helped to rescue from the wanton destruction of the Boche Vandals."[14] Males who were too young or too old to enlist found employment in an expanded labour market and in this way contributed to the war effort.

Indians in the Western provinces also contributed. From Manitoba especially, Indians near The Pas and

Commissioner W. M. Graham (centre)
File Hills Colony, Saskatchewan. (Public Archives of Canada)

Nick King of the Blood Reserve in the One-Horn Headdress he took overseas in the First World War.
(Glenbow Archives)

21

Griswold, joined up in significant numbers. Several bands, such as the Waywayseecappo Band at Rossburn, Manitoba, were generally against participation.[15] From the File Hills Indian agricultural settlement in south-east Saskatchewan and from the Cote Band located near Fort Qu'Appelle, the enlistment rate was quite high.

For protection or perhaps good luck, some native recruits took a crucifix, rosary beads or a lucky coin with them overseas. A few took more traditional charmed items, particularly feathers. A few even packed a complete set of buckskin clothes. Nick King of the Blood Reserve in Alberta took the famous one-horn headdress as this was considered very powerful war medicine. Someone in Europe apparently took a great liking to the headdress for it was never brought back.

The experience of serving overseas had a noticeable effect. Some learned to speak, read and write English for the first time. A few took brides from the British Isles. As a result of their First World War experiences, the Blackfoot, for example, incorporated the name "pointed helmets" for Germans into their language.

Several hundred soldiers were recruited from the Indians of British Columbia. One of the Okanagan Indians, Private George McLean, was awarded the Distinguished Conduct Medal in recognition of his action during the Battle of Vimy Ridge.

> For conspicuous gallantry and devotion when dealing with enemy snipers. Single-handed he captured nineteen prisoners, and later, when attacked by five more prisoners, who attempted to reach a machine gun, he was able, although wounded to dispose of them unaided, thus saving a large number of casualties.

After the war, he became a fireman in the Vancouver area. Private Edwin Victor Cook, from Alert Bay, British Columbia, of the 7th Battalion, was awarded the DCM. He was killed in the latter months of the war. Private Daniel Pearson, of the Metlakatla Band located near Prince Rupert, received the Military Medal for his actions in the fighting for Hill 70 late in August 1917. He died of pneumonia, October 15, 1917, and was buried in Etaples Military Cemetery in France. A good number of Indians from British Columbia saw service in pioneer battalions and forestry units.

Rates of enlistment differed among the Indians of British Columbia as in the rest of Canada. Most of the Indians in the Prince Rupert district showed little interest in enlisting or in supporting the war effort as a result of "unsettled conditions surrounding the land policy of the government."[16] Many of the native peoples in more remote locations, such as the Northwest Territories, were unaware of the war and were more concerned with their daily subsistence. In places where their health was quite poor, only a few could meet the physical requirements.

Although precise figures are unavailable, archival records reveal a significant incidence of discharge among Indians from remote areas owing to sickness, particularly in the First World War. It seems that lack of previous contact with white communities made them more susceptible to white men's viruses. Those

An Indian in the Canadian Forestry Corps, United Kingdom. (Public Archives of Canada)

engaged in recruiting natives north of the 60th parallel in Canada still find low immunity to be prevalent.

Two Largely Indian Battalions

114th Battalion

Many members of the Six Nations from the Brantford area enlisted voluntarily in the 114th Battalion, nick-named "Brock's Rangers". The 114th was authorized December 22, 1915. Recruits joined from Haldimand County as well as from the Six Nations Reserve. A considerable number of Iroquois also came from Caughnawaga and St. Regis. Some 350 Indians in all joined the battalion. A few received commissions. Two crossed tomahawks surmounted

Badge of the 114th Battalion (Canadian War Museum)

by an Indian head were chosen as the regimental badge. The 114th, like many other battalions, was broken up about a year later in England and its members were dispersed as reinforcements, some of the Indian members going to the 107th Battalion.

Attached to the 114th Battalion was a thirty-piece band of whom most were Indians from the Six Nations Reserve at Ohsweken. The band followed the battalion to Camp Borden and then overseas to England where it toured for ceremonial purposes. A feature of their concert was Indian war dances performed by some of the bandsmen. In 1917 the band was broken up and many of its members were assigned to combat units.

107th Battalion

More than 500 Indians of many different tribes from all across Canada[17] served in the 107th Battalion. Raised in December 1915 in the Winnipeg area, with the support of the Indian Department, this battalion was at first envisaged as an all-Indian unit with white officers. The person largely responsible for raising and recruiting the battalion was the tall and stately, Glen Lyon Campbell, Chief Inspector of

Indian Agencies in the Department of Indian Affairs at Winnipeg. He was fluent in several native languages and had served in the militia during the North-West Rebellion.[18] Lieutenant Colonel Campbell, a non-Indian, became the first officer commanding the battalion in July 1915 and he helped train the men in Canada and England. The other commissioned officers were also white to the best of my knowledge.

Quite soon it was found that there were insufficient Indian recruits to make the 107th Battalion an entirely Indian unit so non-Indian reinforcements were added. The battalion embarked at Halifax on September 18, 1916, and arrived at Liverpool a week later. On February 1, 1917, the unit was converted to a pioneer battalion and on February 25 it crossed to Boulogne.[19] It saw action in France and Belgium under Lieutenant Colonel Campbell. At Hill 70, near Lens, in August 1917 the 107th Battalion dug communication trenches under intense fire between the Canadian and German front lines. Casualties were heavy. During the assault on Hill 70, Private Andrew William Anderson from Punnichy, Saskatchewan, a Cree in the 107th Pioneers, earned the Military Medal. The citation reads:

> On August 15, 1917, Private Anderson accompanied Major Warren across 'No Man's Land' under exceptionally heavy fire. He assisted in taping out the communication trenches to be constructed and although shells were bursting all around, bravely carried on with his

Badge of the 107th Battalion. (Canadian War Museum)

> task. His utter disregard of danger was a magnificent example of coolness and determination. Later, during the work, he carried wound-

ed out of shell fire, and throughout the engagement was of invaluable assistance to the working party and to the wounded.

Colonel Campbell, who received the Distinguished Service Order, died of illness at the front on October 20, 1917.[20] In 1918 the 107th Pioneer Battalion was disbanded and its members were absorbed into a brigade of engineers.[21] Thus came to a quiet end a unit with significant numbers of Indians.

Should there have been a Canadian Indian battalion in the Great War? Practical considerations such as distance, rivalries among the various Indian groups in Canada and recruitment problems would have made it a difficult if not impossible undertaking. One's view as to whether this country's military force should serve as a cultural melting pot may affect each reader's opinion.

Maori battalions were formed in New Zealand in both World Wars, notably in World War II. In contrast, the Americans integrated Indians within the army. They followed this course as a result of an unsuccessful experiment in 1892 of separate Indian infantry and cavalry units in the regular army.[22] A special study was undertaken in 1918 by Lieutenant John R. Eddy, a former agent with the northern Cheyennes, as to the best utilization of the Indians in the American forces. It recommended "that recognition of the scouting qualifications of the Indian be officially indicated with a view to having his services more generally made use of in the battalion scout platoons.[23] This proposal was never acted upon. The overwhelming view in the United States among both whites and Indians was in favour of integrating the American Indian among the white units.[24]

Thus two battalions, the 114th and 107th, which had large concentrations of Indian recruits, were not notably successful. However, many soldiers of native ancestry shone individually within the various battalions as excellent scouts and snipers. This was in keeping with their traditional way of life and culture where individual feats of heroism in battle were held in high esteem. Life in the forces helped promote integration as well as assimilation.

Indian Officers

In the First World War very few Indians received commissions. Lack of formal education and military experience in the militia were the main factors. Those who became officers commanded the respect of their fellow officers as well as the men who served under them.

O. M. Martin

The highest appointment ever attained by an Indian in either World War was brigadier. Oliver Milton Martin (1893-1968), a Mohawk from Brantford, Ontario, went overseas in 1916 as a lieutenant in the 114th Battalion. He served in France and Belgium until seconded for duty with the Royal Flying Corps in September 1917. Remaining in the Non-Permanent Active Militia after the war, he rose to the command of the Haldimand Rifles, an appointment he held from 1930-37 and on its reorganization became commanding officer of the Dufferin and Haldimand Rifles, a position he held until shortly after the outbreak of the Second World War. In July 1940 he was appointed to the command of the 13th Infantry Brigade, first as a colonel and from May 1941 as a brigadier.

The following September he was appointed to command an Infantry Brigade of the 6th Division and in May 1945 to the 7th Division. In civil life between the wars, he was a teacher and a school principal in Toronto and a magistrate in the County of York following the war.

Hugh John McDonald

The story of Hugh John McDonald is of particular interest to the Yukon. His grandfather, Neil McDonald, had been an employee of the Hudson's Bay Company who settled on the Red River. Neil's son, Robert, became a priest in the Anglican Church. After serving from 1836 to 1862 among the Ojibway at Whitedog north of Kenora, Robert went north, spending some forty years as a pioneer missionary in the Yukon and Mackenzie River district. He translated the Gospels and the book of Common Prayer into one of the Athapaskan languages and both translations were published by the British and Foreign Bible Society. In 1876 he became archdeacon of the Mackenzie River district. The following year he married one of his converts, Julia Smith, a full-blooded Indian of the area. They had four sons and three daughters. Archdeacon McDonald died in Winnipeg in 1913.

One son, Kenneth, joined the Royal Navy. Another, Hugh John, enlisted in the Canadian Expeditionary Force. At Passchendaele, as a private soldier in the 49th Battalion, he earned the Military Medal:

> For conspicuous gallantry and devotion to duty during the operation from night October 28/29 to October 31st/November 1st, in which the battalion carried out the

attack on the German line in the vicinity of Passchendaele Ridge. This man was the only runner left in this company after the attack and on two occasions proceeded through an intense enemy barrage with messages to the company on his flank gaining and giving information of great value. For 40 hours he worked incessantly and assisted the stretcher bearers in dressing and evacuating the wounded. Throughout the action he exhibited qualities of coolness, initiative and endurance of the highest type and his value to his company was immeasurable.

By virtue of outstanding service in the field, McDonald was commissioned. He was wounded twice, and died of influenza and pneumonia in England.

Gilbert Clarence Monture

A descendant of Joseph Brant, Gilbert Clarence Monture was born in a log cabin in 1869, in Tuscarora Township, Brant County, Ontario. In 1914 he entered Queen's University to study mining and metallurgy. On December 5, 1917, "Slim", as he was known, enlisted as a gunner in the 72nd (Queen's) Battery of the Canadian Engineers with the rank of lieutenant on May 1, 1918, and a few months later went overseas. A lung infection later forced him into hospital and out of action.

Following the war, Monture worked a year, then resumed his studies at Queen's. In 1923, he joined the federal Department of Mines. In view of the rise of fascism and Mussolini's invasion of Ethiopia, he joined the militia in 1935. Up until 1940, Monture held a commission as lieutenant in the 3rd Field Company, Royal Canadian Engineers in Ottawa. He wanted to see action overseas but his age and injury to a hand from a mining accident prevented this. Monture was loaned to the Department of Munitions and Supply, where he acted as executive assistant to the Metals Controller. In January 1944 he began work as Canadian executive officer at the Combined Production and Resources Board in Washington, DC. For his services here, he was awarded the Vanier Medal of the Institute of Public Administration of Canada in 1966 and became an Officer of the Order of Canada in 1972. Dr. Monture also devoted much time to his people. Although Gilbert Monture died in 1973, his life will be remembered as an example worthy of emulation not by Indians but by all other Canadians.

Lieutenant G.C. Monture, Canadian Engineers, c. 1919. (Mrs. A. Malloch)

J.D. Moses and J.R. Stacey

Two Indian officers of the 114th Battalion later joined the air force. Lieutenant James David Moses of the 114th from Ohsweken, a school teacher on the Six Nations Reserve, was seconded to the Royal Flying Corps as an observer on September 3, 1917. He served with Nos. 98 and 57 Squadrons. Moses was shot down by anti-aircraft fire over enemy lines in France on April 1, 1918, and died of wounds in a German prison camp. Lieutenant John Randolph Stacey of Caughnawaga, who had been a successful customs broker in Toronto before the war, was a friend of Billy Bishop. A promising pilot in No. 86 and later 85 Squadron, he was killed in a flying accident in England on April 8, 1918.

Alexander Smith

A son of a Six Nations Chief, he went on to become an officer. Lieutenant Alexander George Edwin Smith of the 20th Battalion, was awarded the Military Cross "for conspicuous gallantry in action" on the Somme in October 1916. "He proceeded with a party of bombers and captured an enemy trench and fifty prisoners, displaying the greatest courage throughout. He was twice buried by shells but stuck to his post.'' Smith was three times wounded and made an officer of the Order of the Black Star of Benin, a French decoration. Upon his return to Canada, Captain Smith was made adjutant of a Polish training battalion at Niagara-on-the-Lake. The trainees, although part of the Polish Army, were under Canadian command, with the Department of Militia suplying the training staff and support services. Smith subsequently became a chief of the Six Nations. A son, Harry, achieved fame as an actor under the name of Jay Silverheels. He is perhaps better known as Tonto, the Lone Ranger's faithful Indian scout and companion.

Notable Native Soldiers

In this section I have included a brief selection of those who did not receive commissions yet were either well known or later gained some notoriety.

Alexander Decoteau

The son of a brave who fought against the Canadian militia in 1885, Alexander Decoteau was born near Battleford on the Red Pheasant Reserve, Saskatchewan, in December 1887. For his racing prowess, usually middle distance, he earned a place on the Canadian Olympic team that went to Stockholm in 1912. Alex left his position as a sergeant in the Edmonton Police Department in April 1916 to enlist in the Canadian Expeditionary Force. While overseas, he, like many others, experienced the misery of trench fever and of lonely, sleepless nights when he would think about family and home. On the morning of October 30, 1917, he was killed in the attack on Passchendaele Ridge.

Grey Owl

The story of Grey Owl, who was not born an Indian, is nevertheless of interest. Early in the war he enlisted in the Canadian infantry under his English name, George S. Belaney. On April 24, 1916, he was wounded in the right foot and the fourth toe had to be amputated. After further operations he was discharged with a twenty per cent disability pension. Grey Owl became a noted writer and lecturer and is remembered as a conservationist, and particularly for his efforts to save the beaver.

Long Lance

Another veteran who doubtfully acquired fame as a full-blooded Indian was Sylvester C. Long. He did have some Indian blood, as did both his parents.

Born in Winston-Salem, North Carolina in 1890, he assumed full Indian identity to escape the humiliation of being treated as a "colored" in the American south. Following attendance at Carlisle Indian Residential School in Pennsylvania and St. John's Military Academy in New York State, he moved north and joined the Canadian Expeditionary Force in 1916 in Montreal under the name Sylvester Long Lance. He fought at Vimy Ridge and was wounded twice in 1917. Subsequently, as a writer with the *Calgary Herald, Vancouver Sun* and *Winnipeg Tribune,* Long Lance specialized in stories about Indians. He later found employment as secretary and

S.C. Long Lance in the uniform of an officer of the 38th Battalion. The highest rank he achieved was that of acting staff sergeant. (Glenbow Archives)

bodyguard to Anita Baldwin, a wealthy heiress in California. In 1932 he committed suicide on her estate because of personal difficulties.

Joe Keeper

Several Indians played a conspicuous part in recreational activities behind the lines. As part of the Dominion Day celebration in 1918 the Canadian Corps held a sports day north of Tincques, a village fourteen miles west of Arras. In both the one-mile and the three-mile race, Corporal Joseph Benjamin Keeper (1886-1971), from Norway House in

Manitoba, was the winner. The more famous Tom Longboat, however, came first in the eight-mile run from Vimy Ridge to Arras and back. Keeper was a middle distance runner (one to ten miles) and a member of the Canadian Olympic team at Stockholm in 1912. For his courage on the battlefield, he was awarded the Military Medal.

Tom Longboat

Tom Longboat, the long-distance runner from Six Nations of the Grand River Reserve, enlisted in 1916 as a private in the 180th Battalion, a Toronto unit, at

Private Tom Longboat (right) buys a paper from a French newsboy. (Public Archives)

age 30. He served overseas mainly with the 107th Pioneer Battalion and the 2nd Battalion, Canadian Engineers. He was wounded while serving as a despatch runner. On one occasion he was reported dead and his wife re-married. Following the war, he married another woman, Martha Silversmith, who bore him four children. Tom held a variety of jobs but worked mainly for the streets department of the City of Toronto. In 1945 he retired and eventually moved back to the reserve. There he died in 1949.

Francis Misinishkotewe

I have been informed by several native Canadians that Private Francis Misinishkotewe, an Ojibway from Manitoulin Island, won the Russian equivalent of the Victoria Cross, Britain's highest award for valour. This is not so. Imperial Russian orders and decorations for Canadian troops were allocated by the British government. Who should receive them, however, was decided by Canadian authorities. Private Francis Misinishkotewe was, in fact, given

the Cross of Saint George, but only 4th class, for heroism in France. More than one hundred Canadians were also given this award. Many of the Canadian soldiers who received it had eastern European names, and it may be that some official believed that "Misinishkotewe" was such a name.

Henry Norwest

Perhaps the most successful sniper among the Canadian Indians, if not on the entire Western Front, was Private Henry Norwest, MM and bar, of Cree ancestry from Alberta. Norwest was finally credited with 115 observed hits and possibly more.[25] A short, powerfully built man, he was noted for his patience and calmness of manner even under enemy fire. Norwest was killed on August 18, 1918, while endeavouring to locate a nest of enemy snipers. Sergeant P.A. Blain described him as:

> reserved rather than effusive. I met a great many Indians before the war, but 'Ducky' (a nickname given Norwest for *ducking* the girls while on leave in London) seemed to stand above them all. He was one of the finest men I ever met.[26]

Norwest gravesite. (Glenbow Archives)

Other Native Snipers

Several First World War veterans have mentioned to me how well native snipers performed. Although names are unknown or forgotten, all accounts mention the excellent adaptation of hunting and fieldcraft skills to the fighting. Often by carefully camouflaging themselves they were able to blend so well into the terrain that their own comrades were unable to detect their movements across No Man's Land.

Only bits of information have endured about some Indian snipers. Private Philip McDonald, although an Iroquois from St. Regis, enlisted with the 90th (Winnipeg Rifles) Battalion. He served overseas with the 8th Battalion. McDonald is reputed to have killed forty Germans as a sharpshooter. He was himself killed on 3 January 1916. Another noted sniper, Patrick 'Paddy' Riel from Port Arthur, a grandson of Louis Riel, amassed 28 notches on his rifle. Also a member of the 8th Battalion, he was killed in action eleven days later. Other notable Indian snipers were brothers, Peter and Sampson Comego of the Alderville Band, Roseneath, Ontario and George Stonefish, a Delaware of Moraviantown, Ontario.

Reports and accounts in the war diaries of the First World War acknowledge the excellence of Indians as snipers, observers. scouts and members of raiding parties. As a result of their record as scouts and snipers, Indians in both Canada and the United States found themselves at times being initially stereotyped into this type of role in the Second World War. Many, however, gladly accepted this type of assignment.

Francis Pegahmagabow

The most highly decorated Indian of the Great War was Francis Pegahmagabow, an Ojibway born in 1891, a member of the Parry Island Band in Ontario. Orphanned while a child he was raised by relatives of the nearby Shawanaga Band. When war broke out Pegahmagabow joined the 1st Battalion (Western Ontario Regiment) in 1914. While at Valcartier with the 1st Division, he decorated his army tent with traditional symbols, including a deer, the symbol of his clan. He claimed to his comrades, who nicknamed him 'Peg' or 'Peggy', that a medicine bag presented to him by an elder would give him a charmed life overseas. He was right. On Mount Sorrel in 1916, he helped capture large numbers of prisoners. At Passchendaele on 6-7 November 1917, and at Amiens on 8-11 August 1918, he again displayed heroic qualities. His exploits brought the Military Medal and two bars.

Like the other scouts and snipers, Francis Pegahmagabow was a rugged individualist. His iron nerves, patience and superb marksmanship helped make him an outstanding sniper who relished hunting enemy snipers. Accounts of the number of his kills vary to as high as 378! Some describe his record as being the greatest of any Allied sniper on the Western Front.

After the war, he returned to live on Parry Island. From 1921 to 1925, Pegahmagabow served as Chief of the Parry Island Band and as a councillor from 1933 to 1936. His experience overseas gave him an increased interest in the culture of his people and while a chief, he encouraged the preservation of traditional beliefs, customs and skills. He died in 1952 from a respiratory ailment.[27]

John Shiwak

I have not come across any Inuit from the Northwest Territories who were in the Canadian forces in either World War. There were, however, a small number of Inuit from the Labrador coast of Newfoundland, then not part of Canada, who served overseas. These men had various degrees of familiarity with the white man and his culture. They enlisted out of a spirit of patriotism and adventure.

One of the Inuit who enlisted and fought overseas

Corporal Francis Pegahmagabow, 1st Battalion, thrice awarded the Military Medal. (Duncan Pegahmagabow)

28

in the First World War from Labrador,* was John Shiwak from Rigolet, north-east of Happy Valley -Goose Bay. Following training in Great Britain, he was among the reinforcements sent to replace members of the Royal Newfoundland Regiment killed at Beaumont Hamel. He became the regiment's leading sniper. Lance Corporal Shiwak was killed in action at age 28, near Marcoing, France, 20 November 1917. His skill as a scout and observer as well as good nature was sorely missed.

Fredrick Frieda (also Friede)

I was able to obtain only bits of information about those of Inuit ancestry who went overseas. Surviving details of Fred Frieda's story are representative of others. Of Inuit and some white ancestry, he was born near Hopedale, Labrador, in October 1895. His family surname was given by Moravian missionaries whose predecessors had arrived at Hopedale in 1782. Although war was not an inherent part of his way of life, Fred Frieda enlisted in the 1st Newfoundland Regiment and fought overseas in Flanders. After the war, he returned home and resumed his life as a hunter and trapper. Like recent Viet Nam and other combat veterans, he had some horrible memories of the fighting that were often revived when he dreamed or drank. He was married twice, once just after the end of the war and again about 1932, a year after the death of his first wife. Throughout his life, Fred Frieda displayed traits such as excellent marksmanship and coolness under dangerous circumstances, characteristics that had enabled him to survive the war. The Canadian Rangers, a Reserve Militia unit, was formed in the North after the Second World War. Frieda joined in 1951 and became a sergeant in 1953. He died 24 March 1970, survived by one son, William.

The Armistice

By 1918, war weariness was growing in Canada. The civilian population, particularly those with relatives overseas, wanted their loved ones safely back. This trend was also evident among the Indian population as evidenced by growing numbers of requests through the Indian Department to have sons or husbands returned home. The Principal of St. Paul's School, Macleod, Alberta, the Reverend Samuel H. Middleton wrote to Duncan Campbell Scott, the Deputy Superintendent General of Indian Affairs in Ottawa, on 3 September 1918, pointing out

*Other examples of Inuit or those with some Inuit ancestry from Labrador who enlisted, mainly in the Royal Newfoundland Regiment, were: John Blake, Tom Flowers, Abraham Ford, John Ford, Tim Ford, Fredrick Frieda, Jourdan Goudie (Indian), Job Lane,

that the death of Albert Mountain Horse had aroused bitter emotions on the Blood Reserve. He noted that other young men from the reserve, Joe and Mike Mountain Horse, Nick King and George Coming-Singer, members of the 50th Battalion, had all been wounded. He warned of his fear of the possible consequences if they were killed.[28] Fortunately, the war soon came to an end and the ordeal was over.

On 11 November 1918, at 11 a.m., hostilities and the sound of firing ceased. Wild enthusiasm marked the occasion in every Allied city. What the future would bring was uncertain, but for good or ill the old pre-war world had disappeared forever. Indian

Lance Corporal John Shiwak poses for a photo in Highland dress at Ayr, Scotland. (Royal Canadian Legion, Happy Valley, Labrador)

Joseph Michelin, Robert Michelin, Abia Millik, Austin Pardy, Manuel Pardy, Jonathan Saimat, Freeman Saunders, and William Winters.

A group of Stonies and friends at Armistice celebrations, west of High River, Alberta, November 1918. (Glenbow Archives)

soldiers faced an especially difficult period of readjustment to civilian life. Most had experienced a totally different world and way of living.

Following the Armistice, the Canadian troops learned that they were to march to the Rhineland as part of the British Army of Occupation, a distinction they prized highly. On the morning of 4 December the leading units reached the German frontier but the more publicized crossing of the Rhine at Cologne and Bonn nine days later was considered more significant. One of those who crossed at Cologne was Private Paul Michel, 8th Battalion, a member of the Gull Bay Reserve on Lake Nipigon, Ontario. He wrote: "The towns and cities are fine. I go to Cologne to-morrow. The people look sour, but who cares."[29] After several months of garrison duty, the Canadian troops were gradually sent home and demobilized. With demobilization, Indian veterans would face quite a difficult period of adjustment.

Cadet Corps

There has been a long affiliation of Indian schools on the reserves and cadet corps. The first corps was organized by Samuel Middleton on the Blood

Reserve consisting of 25 boys aged five to eighteen. In spite of the objection from the Indian Agent, Middleton took the corps to Calgary to a province-wide cadet camp. The Indian boys triumphed over the white boys, carrying off major honours. The motto of the corps is *Mokokit-ki-aikakimit* meaning "be wise and persevere". Soon after this corps had the honour of forming the guard of honour for the Prince of Wales when he visited Macleod in October 1919. Soon other schools on Indian reserves began to form their own cadet corps. Indian cadet corps became a major source of Indian recruits during the Second World War.

School Cadets, Blood Reserve, Alberta, 1920. (Anglican Church of Canada Archives)

Conscription

At the beginning of the war, all Canadian soldiers were volunteers. By the early summer of 1916, however, the needs of industry and agriculture, which had expanded greatly under the stimulus of war, brought increasing demands on manpower and the recruiting situation began to deteriorate. Then came the Somme, with its enormous toll, followed by a falling-off of voluntary enlistments. By May 1917, the Prime Minister, Sir Robert Borden, had made up his mind that the voluntary system must give way to compulsory military service. Canada's effort, he felt, must not falter, even if there had to be conscription to maintain the strength of the Canadian Corps. After a bitter debate in Parliament the Military Service Act, providing for compulsory service, became law on August 29, 1917. The provisions of the Military Service Act applied to all male British subjects in Canada, especially those between 20 and 45 years. Men were placed in six classes. The first to be summoned were young men, either unmarried or childless widowers between the ages of 20 and 34. Tribunals were also to be appointed to deal with individual claims of exemption and to hear appeals. Those specifically exempted were conscientious objectors, all clergy, and members of the Mennonite or Doukhobor communities. To obtain exemption, treaty Indians were required to register. This was to prevent whites from escaping military service by posing as Indians. As registration had to be completed before November 10, 1917, letters of protest came from Indian Agents pointing out that many young Indians were out on the hunt and did not know about the requested exemptions. On many reserves all eligible males had already enlisted. On November 16 the Military Service Council extended the time for registration for Indians to February 1, 1918.

Letters from some Indians objected to both registration and compulsory service, claiming exemption by treaty right. Band chiefs argued that as Indians were considered wards of the Crown and without the right to vote, they should be exempt.[30] On January 17, 1918, an Order-in-Council (PC 111) was passed officially exempting treaty Indians from combatant duties. Indian agents could make out the application for exemption and a certificate of exemption would be forthcoming. Treaty Indians who had enlisted between the Military Service Act and the Order-in-Council permitting their exemption could apply for a discharge.[31] The question of Eskimos did not even arise. Compulsory national registration took place on June 22, 1918, for all men and women over sixteen in Canada. In spite of protests, treaty Indians were compelled to register.[32]

To strengthen its position in the general election of December 1917, the Borden government had passed the Military Voters Bill. The bill defined military electors as including all British subjects on active service in the Canadian forces as well as recent immigrants to Canada who were serving in any forces of Britain or her allies. The bill also covered treaty Indians in the forces. These Indians could vote in a polling station closest to the reserve or if this were not feasible, a polling station could be set up on the reserve[33] without their losing treaty status. This right applied to subsequent federal elections. Treaty Indian veterans of the Second World War also had similar voting privileges.

Race Relations

The Indians and Metis who fought in the Great War did so to help bring about a better world. Having survived the war, however, many continued to live at the bottom of the economic ladder. One can imagine the despair some experienced as the years passed and their lot did not improve, especially in comparison to their white colleagues.

For the most part, Indians and whites in military service were on amicable terms as all were experiencing the same treatment and conditions. As the need for men overseas grew during World War 1, efforts were made to recruit Indians into non-combatant forestry and railway construction battalions. Indians were frequently assigned to special companies in these units. On the west coast, whites in British Columbia strongly objected in March 1917 when it was proposed that Indians there be amalgamated into their units. In the Yukon, several Indians were not allowed to go with their first contingent "on account of race prejudice on the part of other enlisted men."[34] This rebuff discouraged other Yukon Indians from enlisting. Increased contact in the armed forces sometimes helped to promote tolerance and lessen bigotry. There was, however, none of the racial conflict such as occurred between Negro and Caucasian troops in the United States.

The impression given by Duncan Campbell Scott, Deputy Superintendent General of Indian Affairs and other officials, was that all Indians were enthusiastic about enlisting.[35] However, there was strong opposition to recruitment and conscription at Ohsweken and bitterness at their treatment by the government voiced by the Indians at St. Regis and Oka and other reserves.[36] Where tension existed between the local white population and native communities, such as on Manitoulin Island, it was necessary to send in recruiting officers from another area or else the response would have been entirely negative.[37]

Early in the war a separation allowance of $20.00 a

month was granted to the wives and families of rank and file soldiers. From April 1, 1915, all those who were paying separation allowance were required to assign one-half of their pay to dependents. Unlike the rest of the population, dependents of Indian soldiers on reserves were supervised by the Indian Agent to ensure that the money received was wisely spent.

The absence of husbands overseas during the First World War did result in tension between Indian and white communities in newly settled areas as Indian families with the financial help of their husbands could now move off the reserves. An example is the furor aroused by the settlement of Indian women and children in Elk Lake, Ontario. Traditional prejudices of the white community came to the fore.

"Ladies Institute to Mayor of Elk Lake

The ladies of the town in general pray that Your Worship take what action you deem necessary towards the removal of the James Bay Indians before we have an epidemic in the town; also a number of them are morally unfit to be residents of Elk Lake.

Yours truly,

Elk Lake Ladies Institute
(Mrs. J.W. Rodie)

An Indian reply to the Ladies of the Institute

We have all heard the ladies of Elk Lake wants to remove us from Elk Lake. If the ladies wants to find out who brought us to Elk Lake, ask Mr. McCarthy [the recruiting officer and local police magistrate]... We are not going to move out for any letter from the Ladies' Institute. We promised to stay in Elk Lake until our husbands come home and James Bay Indians are just as clean as anyone in Elk Lake. By rights all white men should have went to the front before the Indians.

From the James Bay Indians, Elk Lake, Ontario."[38]

The James Bay Indians remained.

But all feelings towards Indians were not all negative. The contribution by Indians to the Great War did evoke some sympathy as to their situation as evinced by letters to newspapers. One white veteran of the 52nd Battalion wrote to the *Port Arthur News Chronicle:*

...These boys had nothing to fight for. Indians had no vote and could not hold land. Their people, however, have a treaty with the government of Upper Canada made at the Sault in 1850 by which they agreed to give all their right, title and interest in the lands from Batchawana Bay to Pigeon River, excepting a few reserves on which they agreed to live. The government on their part agreed to pay each Indian a small annuity—$4.00 each—and to allow the Indians free and full right to hunt and fish over the lands then ceded and the waters thereof. The Indians kept their part of the treaty. The Dominion government pays the annuity of $4.00 per head but the Ontario government does not recognize the Indians' hunting and fishing rights. As a result the Indian is at the mercy of provincial constables, game wardens and magistrates if he shoots a moose, traps a beaver out of season or sells fish without a license...

During the past three years aged Indians from this district have been fined and imprisoned for having moose meat in their camps. Among these was an old man whose two sons left with the 52nd, one being killed and the other twice severely wounded.

(signed) FAIRPLAY[39]

In remote areas hunting and fishing remained important sources of livelihood. During the fighting Indians received low prices at home as overseas demand dropped. After the war they faced strong competition from white trappers who seriously depleted previously productive areas. In order to acquire a registered trap-line off the reserve Indians were required to surrender their treaty status.

During the First World War, the government undertook to increase agricultural output and a "Greater Production Campaign" was launched. This affected all reserves having farming land. In early 1917 meetings were held on reserves to discuss ways of achieving greater production. Fall fairs were organized on several reserves to help promote agriculture. The campaign was successful for harvests on reserves were reported to be the largest on record.

In 1918 an influenza epidemic spread across Canada affecting one person in every six and causing some 30,000 deaths. The native population was particularly affected. For veterans weakened by war injuries, the virus often proved fatal. Influenza and tuberculosis were a common cause of death among returned wounded Indian veterans. Better housing, particularly in northern communities, would have decreased fatalities.

It became evident in attempts to trace First World War veterans of Indian ancestry who fought overseas that a significant number from more remote areas of Canada died of sickness between the wars. Although they are not included in Appendix B, their military service was likely a contributing factor in their demise and their sacrifice should also be remembered.

During the First World War, drinking was to some extent discouraged in the forces. In the Second World War, it was more accepted. For some native soldiers alcoholism was a serious problem in either conflict. The change from the illegality of alcohol on reserves to its relative availability in the forces proved for some a negative aspect of the military experience. Some returned with an addiction that would cause problems for themselves, their families and their communities for many years.

Conclusion

Canada's war record did much to bring the country to autonomy. By virtue of her part in the war, Canada signed the peace treaties separately and had a seat of its own in the League of Nations. Autonomy came with the Statute of Westminster in 1931. An important step from colony to nation was taken on the bloody torn-up ground that stretched along the Western Front.

The transformation of Canada from a basically agricultural society to one greatly industrialized was also hastened by war. The government introduced "Victory Loans" and various taxes including income tax in 1917, as a means of raising funds to finance Canada's war effort. Treaty Indians on reserves were exempted. Chiefs, bands and Indian patriotic groups helped financially as best they could.

Canada's Indians who had been strongly encouraged to enlist ended up paying a significant toll in killed, wounded and sick. In contrast to the country which made political and economic gains, the lot of the Indian people remained much the same. The sacrifice of killed and wounded achieved very little politically, economically or socially for them.

Several Indians on a reserve north of Lloydminster, Saskatchewan, (Saskatchewan Archives)

Canadian Patriotic Fund poster. (Public Archives of Canada)

34

PART II

BETWEEN THE WARS

Soldier Settlement

After the war, veterans who wanted to go into farming were assisted by the Soldier Settlement Board, which could purchase land for them. Among the lands sold by bands according to the Indian Act and bought by the Board, were Indian reserve lands, some 85,000 acres (see Appendix F), particularly in Saskatchewan, at a cost of one million dollars. Money obtained from these purchases was placed in trust by the Department of Indian Affairs. Some of this money was also distributed to members of the bands.

The person who proved the most successful in securing treaty lands from the Indians for the Board was William Morris Graham. Born in Ottawa he had come west with his family. As a teenager, he entered the department as a clerk at Birtle, Manitoba. In February 1904, he was made an inspector of Indian Agents for the Qu'Appelle district of Saskatchewan and in 1918 became Indian Commissioner for Western Canada.[1] Graham had obtained and held this appointment because he was indirectly related to Arthur Meighen, a future Prime Minister of Canada, who in 1918 had acted as Superintendent General of Indian Affairs.[2]

In February 1918, Graham was given by Order-in-Council (PC 393 of 16 February 1918) authority "to make proper arrangements with the Indians for the leasing of reserve lands" and to manage these lands for "greater production".[3] Reserve land, many thousands of acres, was leased to white farmers for up to five years. This was done to promote greater agricultural production for the war effort. The scheme lasted until 1922. Commissioner Graham also helped to increase significantly the amount of land under cultivation by the Indians.

Newspapers of the day carried stories extolling Graham's work.[4] But not all thought he was behaving properly. J.A. Newnham, the Anglican Bishop of Saskatchewan, wrote an angry letter to Deputy Superintendent General Scott about Graham's treatment of the Sioux Band on the Round Lake or Ochapowace Reserve:

Mr. Graham, who has 'Greater Production' on the brain is intending and hoping to transfer them to some Sioux Reserve near Dundurn, and to hand their Reserve over to Soldier Settlement, or some such thing. I beg to enclose their protest most heartily, and to urge that nothing of the sort be done. They are, though left alone by us and still pagans, a very respectable band: steady and industrious. They have been on that Reserve, or in that district for about 50 years and most of them, perhaps, have been born there and they love their home. The I.D. [Indian Department] is supposed to be anxious to have the Indians take greater interest in farming, and complains that they do not farm more. Surely to seize all the best of the farming land in one reserve after another is not the way to encourage them to be farmers?... He [Graham] would not be in such high favour if you could hear how the Indians and the best Indian Agents speak of him...

Mr. Graham may get the praise for 'Greater Production' but it is the poor Indians who make the sacrifice. Greater Production is good and to be sought in a just and honest way, but it is not the whole of statesmanship. Nearly all our Indian work is suffering here because he seems to have eyes and ears and enthusiasm only for greater production. I trust you will be able to comfort these Sioux and allay their fears, and also to see that Mr.

Graham realizes that his first job is that of 'Indian Commissioner'.[5]

In spite of this letter, Graham managed to acquire land from this reserve for soldier settlement.

In February 1918, the new Department of Soldiers' Civil Re-establishment (later Veterans Affairs) had been created to oversee problems of demobilization. One of the programmes of the department was the soldiers' settlement scheme.

The Soldier Settlement Act of 1919 gave veterans wishing to farm an opportunity to obtain Dominion lands or purchase farms. Under Section 15 of the Soldier Settlement Act "the Minister may issue, free, to any settler a soldier grant for not more than one quarter section, of one hundred and sixty acres..." For Indian veterans in Western Canada, this conflicted with an amendment to the Indian Act of 1906 (RSC 1906, Clause 81, Section 164) which stated:

> No Indian or non-treaty Indian resident in the province of Manitoba, Saskatchewan or Alberta or the Territories shall be held capable of having acquired or of acquiring a homestead or pre-emption right under any Act respecting Dominion lands, to a quarter section...in any surveyed or unsurveyed land in the said provinces or territories...[6]

While a few Indian veterans, mostly from Ontario, did obtain loans and purchase some land outside of their reserves without losing their treaty status, at present, as far as can be determined, only half a dozen grants of free land under the Soldier Settlement Act were given to Indian veterans of the Great War on the Prairies off the reserves.

According to the *Sixth Report of the Soldier Settlement Board of Canada, December 31, 1927*, ..the Department of Indian Affairs had granted loans to 224 Indians, most of them in the Province of Ontario... The Indians mostly had their locations on the reserves... Indian soldier settlers are distributed as follows:

Prince Edward Island	5
Quebec	4
Ontario	184
Saskatchewan	18
Alberta	2
British Columbia	11
	224[7]

Thus, out of some 25,000 soldier settlers to whom loans were granted,[8] only a small number were In-

dian soldier settlers. From surviving records, it is clear that most Indian veterans who wished to take up farming under the Soldier Settlement Act wanted to do so on reserve land. On the Prairies only one in ten who applied was granted a loan and the success rate was poor.[9]

Indian veterans of the Great War also faced discrimination when applying for homesteads on the Prairies. Such was the case of Sam Gagnon, a treaty Indian, from Maniwaki, Quebec, who had lost an eye in the fighting overseas. After the war, he had moved to Fort Assiniboine, Alberta. When applying for a homestead in 1934, he was turned down on the grounds that he was an Indian.[10] As mentioned earlier, the Indian Act barred Indians from such acquisitions.

Thus, under pressure to find suitable agricultural land for its veterans, the federal government had purchased Indian reserve land in the West. This action was politically popular, yet it created ill-feeling among Indian bands in Western Canada that still exists today. For many Indian veterans who had fought for their country, there was much despair when the hopes that many had brought back with them following the war were shattered as they struggled to repay soldier settlement loans and survive economically. The period following the First World War proved to be very difficult

While vocational training was offered to veterans, including Indian veterans disabled by the war, by the Department of Soldiers' Civil Re-establishment, perhaps more should have been done for the other Indian veteans. This was the feeling of Mr. E.R. Tucker, a vocational officer in Sudbury, who felt this type of training should be offered to all Indian veterans.[11]

Pensions

Pensions enabled many families to survive. The officer investigating a dependents' pension claim by the father of James Cope, a Nova Scotian Indian, who enlisted at age 15 and was killed in action in 1918 in France, found the following:

> In accordance with instructions I visited Joseph Cope and Windsor Junction recently. This man occupies a small shack erected on land belonging to a white man. The shack itself is probably one of the worst I have ever had the opportunity of entering. Outside of a small trunk, a blanket and stove, there was no other furniture. The shack is about 8 feet by 10 feet in

size and is constructed of rough inch lumber covered with tar paper on the outside.

Joseph Cope himself suffers chronic muscular rheumatism in the left leg and is partially paralysed in the left arm. He is not able to undertake any physical work and hardly able to walk around.

His wife is dead and his eldest son killed at the front. There are five small children, three of whom were in the house at the time of my visit.[12]

Eventually, Joseph Cope was granted a pension on behalf of his son.

The predicament of wounded Indian veterans varied. One case was that of Richard Lathlin, a trapper from The Pas, Manitoba, a former member of the 2nd Battalion. Lathlin had lost his lower left leg. The Indian Agent wrote to the Department on his behalf. Lathlin claimed his disability pension was insufficient and asked for a grant to help build a decent house and purchase a few cows to improve his predicament. "He would have approached the Soldier Settlement Board for a loan but he doubts he can repay it as he earns practically nothing."[13] A year later, he died as a result of tuberculosis, age twenty-four. His immediate family was provided for by a modest government pension.[14]

Following the war, many Indian veterans returned to previous means of livelihood. In the depression of the 1930's, reduced demand for goods and services made times difficult. Unemployment was particularly high among native labour.

The Thirties proved to be an especially difficult economic period for much of Canada's native people. Drought on the prairies, little demand for forest products, furs, handicrafts, unskilled labour or tourist guides brought about a reduction in already low incomes. Some veterans, such as William Semia, who had a large family to support, managed to survive without relief. Others barely were able to support their families. The Indian Agents for Parry Sound and Manitoulin Island reported that two decorated veterans, Francis Pegahmagabow and Francis Misinishkotewe, were not receiving sufficient relief to adequately support their families. There were many other obscure Indian veterans on reserves also in very difficult economic circumstances.[15] For many native veterans the promise of a better future for which they had fought faded amidst dire poverty both off or on the reserve. For those wishing to remain on their reserve, there were additional problems.

War Veterans' Allowance

During the Depression, treaty Indian veterans did not receive the same assistance as other returned soldiers under the War Veterans' Allowance Act. It was decided in the spring of 1932 that Indian veterans on reserves in need of help were to be treated like other Indians on reserves rather than as veterans.[16] Only enfranchised Indian veterans not living on reserves were entitled to the same benefits as non-Indian veterans. The living allowance of $40 per month for a single and $70 for a married veteran accorded by the War Veterans' Allowance Act was more generous than any assistance of Indian Affairs.[17] Although treaty Indians on reserves had certain benefits, the government should have ensured that Indian veterans on reserves received their rightful share of benefits under the War Veterans' Allowance Act. It was not until 1936 that this policy was changed.[18]

As an example of the financial problems faced by some Indian veterans, I have selected the case of Thomas A. Peltier of Wikwemikong on Manitoulin Island, who was wounded in France and permanently disabled. In 1936 with a pension of $24.00 a month and an income of under $400.00 a year, he had to support a wife and six children ranging from eleven years to three months.

Peltier complained in a letter to the Honourable C.G. 'Chubby' Power, then Minister of Pensions:

...I applied for War Veterans' Allowance in 1934. As far as I could understand I was not qualified for veterans' allowance because I was an Indian and residing on an Indian Reserve, the very same place from where I enlisted when the country needed my services...

It is now when the children are young that they need nourishing food... My wife has been sick for the past four months, which is still more expense and I am never very well, most of the time being troubled with rheumatism, besides my disability...

I have tried to get help at different times but never have been able and this is the reason I am writing you personally. I was always advised to apply to the Indian Agent but there is no use asking for help from a man who has never enlisted during the war, and has no sympathy for returned men.[19]

Fortunately, Peltier's letter had the desired effect for a month later the Indian Agent on Manitoulin Island concluded a report about Peltier and his family to the Secretary, Department of Indian Affairs, with the recommendation that they were "eligible for further assistance".[20]

The Last Post Fund

Even some Indian veterans who died were treated unfairly. The Last Post Fund had been established in 1909 and publicly funded in 1922 to prevent any veteran of active service with His Majesty's forces being buried in a pauper's grave.

The Indian Superintendent at Ohsweken, Lieutenant Colonel C.E. Morgan, strove to ensure equal treatment of Indian veterans on the reserve for veterans' benefits. To the Department of Indian Affairs, he wrote:

> I fail to see why because the deceased returned soldier happens to be an Indian that he should be debarred from the benefits of the Fund which was founded for the benefit of all returned men alike... I would say, with all due respect, that it seems to me that Government Departments who are working in the interests of returned soldiers, are too apt in the case of Indians to attempt to transfer the burden of their responsibility to the Department of Indian Affairs.[21]

In February 1936 a case came to light of a veteran who had died without any money being given a meagre pauper's funeral by Indian Affairs. "Representatives of St. Thomas Branch No. 41 Canadian Legion who attended the funeral reported it a most deplorable affair. The money appropriated by the Department being insufficient to provide a rough box or hearse"[22], contributions by various organizations and individuals being required. Protests revealed that the last Post Fund was only being permitted to pay for the headstone of Indian veterans on reserves.[23] From the late 1920's, the Last Post burial privilege and pension relief fund had been discontinued as Indian veterans on reserves were being treated exclusively as treaty Indians, not as veterans. Taking up the case, J.C.G. Herwig protested on behalf of the Legion's Dominion Command:

> At our Ontario Provincial Convention the following resolution was passed regarding the position of Indian returned soldiers in relation to the legislative and other benefits available to the returned soldier body:

> 'That the Indian War Veterans be placed on the same footing and receive the same benefits as his other Canadian comrades especially in regard to the Last Post Fund, pensioners' relief and Veterans' Allowances, and that the Canadian Legion, B.E.S.L. [British Empire Service League], do everything in their power to bring this about.'

> It appears that in many respects the Indian returned soldier does not receive the same consideration as others, and this has given rise to complaint from some of our Branches. The matter will, undoubtedly, come before our Dominion Convention, but we feel that the conditions reported to us are such that some immediate action should and can quite properly be taken...

> Although the resolution refers to the War Veterans' Allowance, we believe that there is no difficulty in this connection with the administration of the Act insofar as Indians are concerned. But in regard to pensioners' relief, although the Indian returned soldier may receive the rate generally available on reserves, it has frequently been so low that it is altogether out of proportion to that received by other returned soldiers and usually is below minimum rates.

> We are strongly of the opinion that Indian returned soldiers are entitled to the same consideration as others, notwithstanding the fact that they may have a different relation to the State than ordinary citizens...[24]

As a result of these representations policy was subsequently modified so that indigent Indian veterans on reserves received the same benefits as others.[25]

These are only some of the difficulties met by Indian veterans. As well, they faced the same discrimination and problems as other Indian people during this period.

PART III

THE SECOND WORLD WAR

Introduction

During the 1930's, the League of Nations proved ineffectual and the world situation deteriorated. Japanese forces attacked Manchuria. Under Hitler, Germany embarked on a rearmament programme. Italy invaded and conquered Ethiopia. In March 1938 the Nazis took over Austria and in September, at Munich, Hitler was allowed to occupy the Sudetenland in Czechoslovakia. The remainder of Czechoslovakia was occupied by German troops six months later.

In late March 1939 in an attempt to deter Hitler, Britain and France agreed to support Poland in the event of a German attack. Without Russian assistance the Anglo-French undertaking was not militarily realistic, and on September 1, following a "non-aggression" (i.e. non-intervention) pact between Hitler and Stalin, German troops invaded Poland. Britain and France, honouring their undertaking, declared war on Germany on the 3rd. Canada was not involved automatically, as in 1914, but entered the war at the decision of Parliament on September 10.

Indian Favoured Battalions

In the early years of the Second World War, stories abounded in the newspapers demonstrating the support of Canada's Indians for the war effort to help boost public morale and promote Indian recruiting.[1] Indians enlisted mainly in army units in their respective areas.

During the Second World War there were again proposals to establish an all-Indian battalion. This idea was not accepted as it was not considered practical in view of the widely scattered Indian population across Canada and the experience of the First World War. As a result, Indians tended to be even more widely dispersed throughout the Canadian forces than in 1914-1918.

Many and varied would have been the difficulties of maintaining a large all-Indian unit within the Canadian forces. Some of the problems likely would probably have been more acute than those of the Canadian Corps in the First World War or No. 6 (RCAF) Group and No. 425 ("French-Canadian") Squadron in the Second World War. If assignment to a native unit ever became compulsory solely by reason of racial background that policy would have amounted to racial segregation.

To gain some understanding as to what many Indian recruits experienced in both wars imagine if roles and circumstances had been reversed. The adjustment of a white recruit from an urban middle class home in Canada entering an all Indian battalion would not be easy. One wonders if the response of the white community to fight on behalf of the Indian people would have been as strong as the response of Canada's Indians to fight overseas for this country in both World Wars.

Infantry battalions that attracted substantial numbers of native recruits were Princess Patricia's Canadian Light Infantry, the Calgary Highlanders, the Edmonton Regiment, the South Saskatchewan Regiment, the Hastings and Prince Edward Regiment and the Royal Hamilton Light Infantry and, in 1940, the Regina Rifles and the Royal Winnipeg Rifles.

On enlistment, significant numbers of Indians were illiterate. Service in the armed forces was a beneficial experience for those who learned new skills. Lieutenant Colonel Mark Tennant, a former commanding officer of the Calgary Highlanders, tells of Indians coming in from the Blackfoot, Blood, Sarcee, Peigan and Stoney Bands. Nicknames rather than given names are often remembered. A good friend of Colonel Tennant, Leo House from Morley, could barely spell his name when he enlisted in 1939. Private House learned to read and write effectively, completed an Officer Cadet Training Unit course in England, and proved to be a first class officer in North-West Europe. There are other, similar cases such as Lieutenant David Greyeyes from Leask, Saskatchewan. The overwhelming reports I have received speak of the excellent fighting qualities and heroism of Indians in the fighting. One noticeable difference was generally, their personalities tended to be reserved rather than effusive.

Overseas

Indians and Metis saw action in all operations involving Canadian troops in the Second World War-- Hong Kong, December 1941; Dieppe, August 19, 1942; Sicily, July-August 1943; Italy, September 1943-February 1945; and North-West Europe, June 1944-May 1945.

Battles and Campaigns

The experience of the Canadian Army overseas in the Second World War differed significantly from that of the First World War. From 1914-1918, the British Isles served as a base for operations in France and Belgium. The First Canadian Contingent landed in England in October 1914 and crossed to Flanders in February 1915 where it was soon in battle. Most Canadians in Britain at a later date were those wounded, on leave, in advanced training, or in special non-combatant units such as the Forestry Corps. In contrast, the greater part of the Canadian Army was in the United Kingdom until the summer of 1944 without seeing action. The long period of inaction in Britain was frustrating and a severe test of morale and discipline to Indians and non-Indians alike. Like their comrades, Canadian Indians in the forces experienced everything from British pubs to Brussels sprouts to the Blitz. In both World Wars, full-blooded Canadian Indians were often regarded with curiosity and fascination by the British public. As well as memories of Britain, some of those of Indian ancestry, such as Norman H. MacAuley of La Ronge, Saskatchewan, brought home British war brides. Mr. MacAuley served as the elected representative for the provincial constituency of Cumberland in northern Saskatchewan from 1975 until he retired in 1982.

Not all casualties were incurred on the field of battle. Many accidents occurred in Canada and overseas. In Britain, the Canadians for the most part faced seemingly endless training and visits by various dignitaries. There were also training accidents. Private Francis Maracle, a Mohawk from the Bay of Quinte, "a most faithful and efficient soldier",[2] lost his life by accidentally stepping on a land mine in the East Wittering area of England while on guard duty during the night 5th/6th March 1942.

One of the friendliest individuals I have come across who served in England during the Second World War was Douglas White, a Labradorian of Inuit and white ancestry from Nain. He was encouraged to serve overseas by his white father, Richard, who had fought in Flanders. Douglas went to England on a convoy and joined the Royal Air Force early in the war. As a leading aircraftman, White became a mechanic servicing Mitchell bombers of No. 320 (Dutch) Squadron. His explanation as to why he ended up with a squadron from The Netherlands was confusion in sound between Netherlands and Newfoundland. White's superiors had heard of The Netherlands but not Newfoundland. Having attended school in St. John's, he did not find England a severe cultural shock. Following the war, he took vocational training and worked as a mechanic on heavy equipment in Labrador. At the time of writing he is a court worker in Nain.

Hong Kong

In September 1941 the British government, having decided to reinforce the Crown Colony of Hong Kong, proposed that Canada provide one or two battalions for that purpose. At the end of the month the Canadian government agreed. The Canadian force disembarked on November 16, 1941. A few weeks later, commencing on 7 December, the Japanese struck at American, British and Dutch possessions in the Far East. At Hong Kong, the Japanese land assault came from the north rather than the sea as provided for in the siting of the coastal guns. Despite a gallant defence, the garrison was overwhelmed.

As prisoners, the survivors experienced treatment worse than anything previously suffered by Canadian servicemen. They were crowded together in unsanitary quarters and denied sufficient food, vitamins, medical supplies and even clothing. They were forced to perform hard physical labour. Liberation did not come until after the Japanese surrender in August 1945.

Among the 2,000 members of the Canadian force sent to Hong Kong, consisting mainly of the Royal Rifles of Canada and the Winnipeg Grenadiers, were at least fourteen Indians and Metis.*

*From New Brunswick came Henry Martin and from Quebec, Patrick Metallic and Frank Methot, who enlisted in the Royal Rifles of Canada. From Manitoba came Max Noel of the Bird Tail Sioux Band; Stanley Frederic Roy Stodgell from Transcona; Oliver Barron, David Chaboyer, Ernest Lavallee and Jean Joseph Anthony, Sioux from St. Laurent, who did not return; Edgar Herbert Baptiste from the Red Pheasant Reserve near Battleford who died of many wounds, and George Badger from the Cote Band, Kamsack, Saskatchewan, who died as a POW in 1943, all of whom were members of the Winnipeg Grenadiers. Private Bertrand C. Moore from Moose Factory and later Cochrane, Ontario, died of pneumonia and beri-beri while a prisoner at Camp Niigata, Japan, three weeks before the end of the war. Private Edward Joseph Morrisseau of the Fort alexander Band died shortly after his return, as did Private Isaac Sanderson, an Indian living in Selkirk, Manitoba.

Dieppe

By the end of 1941, both Russia and the United States were in the war, Allied strength was increasing, and the fear of a German invasion of Britain began to recede. Throughout 1942, Russia, after heavy German onslaughts, insisted on Allied action to ease the pressure. Both the British and Americans agreed that a massive invasion was not feasible at that time. In July, they decided as an alternative to launch a joint North African campaign in the autumn of 1942. This made it desirable to foster German fears of attack in the West, to allay Russian demands, and to gain experience in planning a large amphibious assault on North-West Europe. Such were the origins of the Dieppe raid. The main body of troops taking part were chosen from the 2nd Canadian Division, which had been overseas two years without seeing action. The attack was a costly failure and its necessity is still questioned.

This was the first large scale operation by Canadian troops in France since a brigade of the 1st Division had been in Britanny for 48 hours in June 1940. Allied troops at Dieppe totalled 6,000, of whom 5,000 were Canadians. Most of the Indians who took part in the Dieppe raid on 19 August 1942 did so with the Royal Hamilton Light Infantry (RHLI) and the South Saskatchewan Regiment. At least five treaty Indians are known to have been killed.*

A Metis from St. Ambroise, Manitoba, Private Louis Lamirande, was at Dieppe. Along with about 1,900 other Canadians, he was taken prisoner. The scars on his wrists bear testimony to his hands being tightly bound with ropes. Louis managed to escape and spent the remainder of the war fighting as a guerrilla with a group of partisans. He is now a much sought after duck-hunting guide.

Sicily

On the evacuation of the Germans from Tunisia in May 1943, it was decided that the next step for the Western Allies would be to invade Sicily. Canada would contribute the 1st Infantry Division and 1st Army Tank Brigade. Soon facing the Canadians were troops ensconced on commanding heights of the Sicilian hills. The first serious encounter took place at Grammichele, perched on a ridge some 250 feet above the level of the surrounding country. From Deseronto, Bay of Quinte, Ontario, a Mohawk, Huron Eldon Brant, a member of the Hastings and Prince Edward Regiment, won the Military Medal.

In the battle for Grammichele on 14 July 1943 Private H.E. Brant distinguished himself for his prompt and courageous attack with his Bren gun on an enemy force of approximately 30 men, inflicting severe casualties.

Private H.E. Brant totally

Private Huron E. Brant of the Hastings and Prince Edward Regiment receives the Military Medal from General Montgomery for bravery at Grammichele in Sicily. (Public Archives)

disregarded his own personal safety in the face of very heavy enemy fire and made possible the killing, or capturing of the entire enemy force.[3]

*Private Elmer Joseph Brant, a Mohawk from the Bay of Quinte, fell there. Private Michael Clarence Goulais of the Nipissing Band from Sturgeon Falls, Ontario, was killed at Dieppe as was Lance Sergeant Franklyn Martin from the Six Nations Reserve. Maxwell Jacob King was lost and his brother, Elliott, became a prisoner-of-war. Their father, Frank L. King, had been a "Chief and Councillor" of the Mississaugas of the Credit Band. The late Private King had been married in England and his widow and young son later came to the Reserve. Private Norman Walter Henry of the Credit Band was killed in action when he too landed with the RHLI. A Metis member of the South Saskatchewan Regiment, Private Edward Joseph Poitras also was killed. The latter three fatalities are buried along with most of their comrades at Dieppe war cemetery.
Several Indians, including Private George Obey from the Piapot Band, near Regina, who was with the South Saskatchewan Regiment, became prisoners-of-war. Two Indians from Saskatchewan who emerged unscathed were Private Albert I. Noname, a member of the Piapot Band and Private F.D. Shingoose of the neighbouring Muscowpetung Band.

41

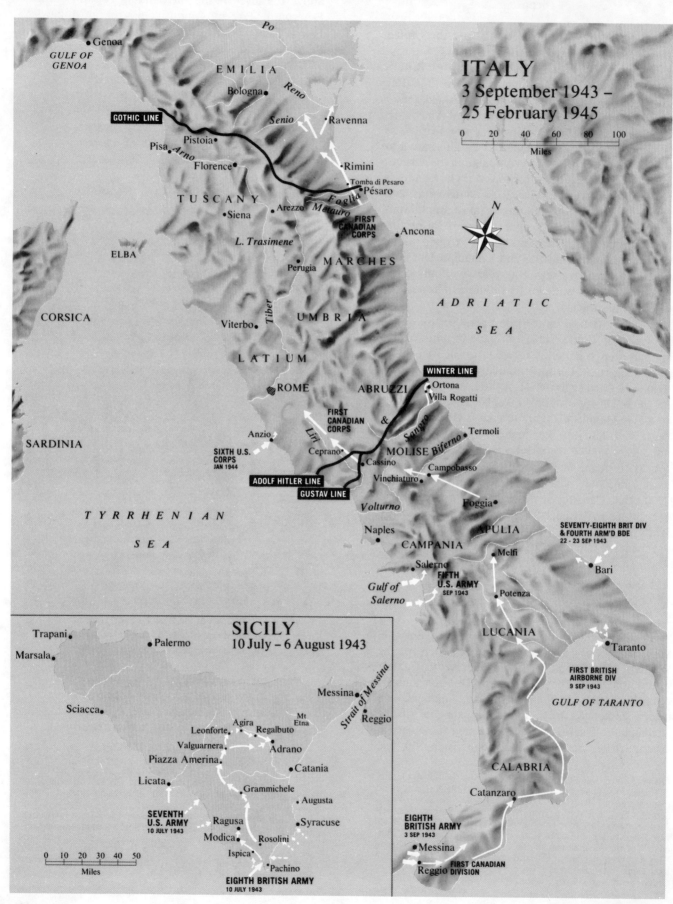

ITALY
3 September 1943 –
25 February 1945

0 20 40 60 80 100
Miles

Po

GULF OF
GENOA

Genoa

EMILIA

Bologna

Reno

Senio

Ravenna

GOTHIC LINE

Pistoia

Pisa

Arno

Florence

Rimini

Tomba di Pesaro

Pésaro

Foglia

TUSCANY

Siena

Arezzo

Metauro

FIRST
CANADIAN
CORPS

Ancona

L. Trasimene

N

ELBA

Perugia

MARCHES

ADRIATIC

CORSICA

Tiber

UMBRIA

SEA

Viterbo

LATIUM

ROME

ABRUZZI

WINTER LINE

Ortona

Villa Rogatti

FIRST
CANADIAN
CORPS

&

Anzio

Liri

Sangro

SIXTH U.S.
CORPS
JAN 1944

Ceprano

MOLISE

Biferno

Termoli

SARDINIA

Cassino

Campobasso

ADOLF HITLER LINE

Vinchiaturo

GUSTAV LINE

Volturno

Foggia

TYRRHENIAN

Naples

APULIA

Melfi

SEA

CAMPANIA

SEVENTY-EIGHTH BRIT DIV
& FOURTH ARM'D BDE
22 - 23 SEP 1943

Salerno

FIFTH
U.S. ARMY
SEP 1943

Potenza

Bari

Gulf of
Salerno

LUCANIA

Taranto

SICILY
10 July – 6 August 1943

FIRST BRITISH
AIRBORNE DIV
9 SEP 1943

GULF OF TARANTO

Trapani

Palermo

Marsala

Messina

Strait of Messina

Sciacca

Reggio

CALABRIA

Leonforte

Agira

Regalbuto

Mt
Etna

Catanzaro

Valguarnera

Adrano

Piazza Amerina

Catania

Licata

Grammichele

Augusta

SEVENTH
U.S. ARMY
10 JULY 1943

Ragusa

Syracuse

EIGHTH
BRITISH ARMY
3 SEP 1943

Modica

Rosolini

Messina

Ispica

0 10 20 30 40 50
Miles

Pachino

EIGHTH BRITISH ARMY
10 JULY 1943

Reggio

FIRST CANADIAN
DIVISION

42

Another Indian who fought in Sicily was Private Daniel Garneau, a member of the band near Wabigoon close to Kenora who had joined the Princess Patricia's Canadian Light Infantry on 30 April 1943. Garneau found himself en route to an unknown destination in late June. On July 10, six days after his twenty-second birthday, he landed in Sicily. Twelve days later, Garneau was killed in the capture of Leonforte, a formidable hill-town. He was buried along with other Canadians killed in Sicily at Agira Cemetery. An Indian in the Seaforth Highlanders of Canada, Frederick Webster, from the Lytton Agency in British Columbia, won the Military Medal.

> During the afternoon of 28 July 1943, the Seaforth of Canada attacked Agira. 'A' Company was ordered to attack and capture a ridge dominating the town from the right. In the course of the attack on the ridge No. 8 Platoon was held up by fire from an enemy machine gun post. Private Webster, a Bren gunner, with complete disregard for his own safety and in the face of heavy machine gun fire, made his way forward to a position from which he could provide covering fire for his section. So accurate and effective was Private Webster's fire that his section was enabled to wipe out the machine gun post and his platoon was able to continue its advance.

Looking back, E.A. 'Smokey' Smith, a Victoria Cross winner from Vancouver, remembered:

> 'Dick' Webster—a brave, brave man who served overseas with me in the Seaforth Highlanders. In England and Italy he was part of our group socially --of course for the first time in his life allowed entrance in pubs, etc. Sadly when he returned to Canada, he was by Canadian law in force at the time, unable to join us in a cocktail lounge or beer parlor. After serving six years in the Canadian army, he was now once again, relegated to the status of what could be termed a second class citizen.

The Italian Campaign

Sicily fell in mid-August and it was then decided to expel the Germans from Italy. The 1st Division and the 1st Canadian Army Tank Brigade crossed the Strait of Messina to the toe of Italy in September and moved northwards. Ortona, at the Adriatic end of the German winter line, fell to the 2nd Infantry Brigade in December 1943 after bitter fighting.

As the Canadians fought their way up the peninsula casualties mounted and the list of those Indians who fell is quite long. It was at the outset of the attack on Ortona that a Metis from Alberta, Sergeant G.A. Campion, was awarded the Military Medal.

> On 22 December 1943 'A' Company of the Loyal Edmonton Regiment were attacking down the main street of Ortona, Italy, supported by a troop of tanks when a mine field was spotted about 30 yards in front of the leading tank. All the infantry were pinned inside buildings by heavy machine gun fire from four guns. Engineers were called forward to clear the field but owing to this fire it was impossible for them to get near the mines.
>
> Sergeant Campion asked permission of his Company Commander to lay a smoke screen. Permission was granted and he gathered a pocket full of smoke grenades from his platoon, ran 30 yards beyond the mine field into the open street and threw his grenades. A perfect smoke screen resulted. He then ran back to his platoon to collect more grenades. In the meantime the engineers, who had not been able to complete their task before the smoke cleared, were driven back by machine gun fire. Returning, Sergeant Campion laid another smoke screen which enabled them to clear the mines and thus allowed the advance to go on.
>
> The distance covered each time under heavy machine gun fire in the open street was approximately 30 yards.
>
> Because of his determination and absolute lack of personal fear on these two occasions, he contributed materially to the success of the operation.

The regimental historian credits this shining example of soldierly behaviour as pointing the way to success at Ortona.[4] Campion was killed in action a few months later. The day following Campion's brave

Private (later Sergeant) J.F. St. Germain of the Edmonton Regiment, while training in England, 1942. (Mrs. M. Plante)

feat, another Metis of the Loyal Edmonton Regiment, Private Peter Versailles, was shot through the heart standing next to his Company Commander, Major J.R. Stone on the main street of Ortona.

After the battle for Ortona, Major (later Colonel) Stone remarked to Sergeant J.F. St. Germain a Metis in the battalion: "What a magnificent job you have done in fighting!" St. Germain looked up and bitterly replied: "Here the boys call me 'the Saint' but back in Canada, I'll be treated just like another poor goddam Indian. I hope I get killed before it is all over." St. Germain was killed in action about a year later. More than forty years later Colonel Stone remembers his "as a brave and most cheerful man, liked by all who served with him."[5]

Following the bloody struggle for Ortona, both sides dug in. In the Ortona salient, from January to April 1944, there was a period of numerous patrols and raids. Corporal Charles Jeremy, a Micmac in the West Novas, demonstrated what could be accomplished by someone who was a crack shot and made excellent use of the terrain. "Jeremy never boasted of his sniping 'kills', but admiring troops placed the figure at 'something like sixty.'"[6] Another able member of this group was Private R.M. Francis, also a Micmac.

But all was not continuous fighting. Leave was granted to give the men a respite. All who served can recall with fondness a favourite spot or a particularly enjoyable leave. A rest centre frequented by native soldiers as well as other Canadians in eastern Italy was the Monastery Inn at Ortona, where a bed, hot meals, clean clothes, a shave and a haircut and a variety of entertainment were provided.

The 1st Canadian Corps broke the Hitler and Gothic Lines of defence in May 1944. Rome fell to the Americans on June 4th.

A Military Cross was won in Italy, north-west of Rimini by an officer of the 1st Field Company, Royal Canadian Engineers, Victor A. Moore. Both his parents were Indians from File Hills who had taken up permanent residence in Regina prior to his birth.

On 13 October 1944, 1st Brigade supported by a squadron of Lord Strathcona's Horse were fighting their way forward along Highway 9, south of Rigossa. Intense rifle, machine gun, mortar and artillery fire had pinned down the leading infantry...and they were unable to advance without tank support. This

Lieutenant V.A. Moore, M.C. Rome, November 1944. (V.A. Moore)

support was unable to get forward on account of large roadblocks built of wine barrels (filled with stone), trees, farm carts, and concrete blocks. An armoured bull-dozer in charge of Lieutenant Victor Alexander Moore was sent forward to deal with these roadblocks. Due to darkness and restricted vision in this machine, the operator was unable to see. Lieutenant Moore, standing for part of the time outside the machine, entirely indifferent to the dangers of his exposed position, guided the bull-dozer throughout its work. The road was eventually entirely cleared and a passage made for tanks, an operation which lasted for nearly three hours, during the whole of which time the enemy continued to bring down both shell and small arms fire on the area. At no time did Lieutenant Moore cease his direction of the operation in order to take cover.

There is no doubt that the perseverance and courage of this officer and his cool and efficient direction of the machine from an exposed position in the face of the greatest difficulties were the main factors in clearing the road. As a result the tanks were able to get forward with the minimum of delay, and with their support the advance of the 1st Brigade was resumed.

(A younger brother, Lloyd George, had perished when HMCS *St. Croix* was torpedoed on September 20, 1943).

During an attack on Bulgaria (village) in mid-October 1944, in north-east Italy near Rimini, "Huron Brant...who had won the Military Medal in Sicily (see page 41), was killed with his entire section when the six men were caught by enfilading machine gun fire in a narrow ditch".[7] Brant lies buried in Cesena War Cemetery nearby.

This brief account mentions only a few of those killed in the Mediterranean. Many others were wounded, some quite seriously. In February 1945 the Canadians were moved to North-West Europe to be re-united with the First Canadian Army.

North-West Europe

D Day

In 1944, with the Germans heavily embroiled in Russia and Italy, the time had come to invade North-West Europe. On June 6 an allied armada of almost 5,500 ships protected by a huge air "umbrella", car-

D Day (Imperial War Museum)

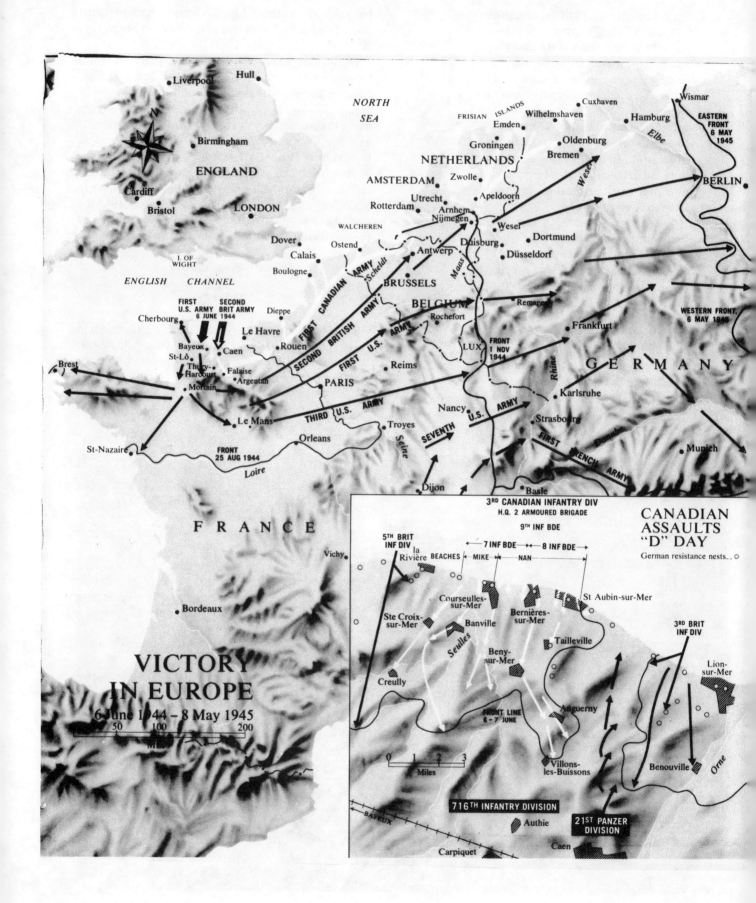

LONDON

I. OF WIGHT

ENGLISH CHANNEL

NORTH SEA

FRISIAN ISLANDS

EASTERN FRONT 6 MAY 1945

NETHERLANDS

AMSTERDAM

WESTERN FRONT; 6 MAY 1945

GERMANY

FRANCE

VICTORY IN EUROPE
6 June 1944 – 8 May 1945

50   100   200
MILES

CANADIAN ASSAULTS "D" DAY

German resistance nests.....

3RD CANADIAN INFANTRY DIV
H.Q. 2 ARMOURED BRIGADE
9TH INF BDE

5TH BRIT INF DIV

7 INF BDE   8 INF BDE

la Rivière   BEACHES   MIKE   NAN

Courseulles-sur-Mer

Bernières-sur-Mer

St Aubin-sur-Mer

3RD BRIT INF DIV

Ste Croix-sur-Mer

Banville

Taileville

Lion-sur-Mer

Seulles

Beny-sur-Mer

Creully

FRONT LINE 6 - 7 JUNE

Anguerny

0   1   2   3
Miles

Villons-les-Buissons

Benouville

Orne

716TH INFANTRY DIVISION

BAYEUX

Authie

21ST PANZER DIVISION

Carpiquet

Caen

ried 50,000 men in five divisions of assault troops, of which one was Canadian (the 3rd Infantry), to the beaches of Normandy. By nightfall, the troops had established a firm beachhead except for one beach precariously held by American troops. One of those killed on D Day was Rifleman Donald Thomas of the Regina Rifles, a member of the Peepeekisis Band, Lorlie, Saskatchewan.

Following the landings, a distinct pattern of fighting could be seen: Allied attacks to enlarge the bridgehead and make room for reinforcements and supplies and violent counter-attacks by the Germans to throw the Allies back into the sea.

Private George T. Munroe M.M., 1944. (Steve Munroe)

Normandy

The Germans mounted an armoured counter-offensive against the Allied beachhead. General Bernard Montgomery's plan was to attract maximum German strength to the Anglo-Canadian front while the Americans would break out of the bridgehead. In the fighting in Normandy between June and August 1944, many Indians and Metis from Canada were killed and wounded.

There were also many acts of bravery. In one such action, Private George Thomas Munroe of the John Smith Band (Birch Hills, Saskatchewan) earned the Military Medal.

During the attack on St. Andre-sur-Orne [19 July], Private Munroe was with a leading platoon of the Queen's Own Cameron Highlanders of Canada. His platoon was held up, in a very exposed position and was unable to get forward without covering fire. Quickly realizing the urgency of the situation, Private Munroe placed himself under heavy machine gun fire and coolly commenced to give covering fire so that his platoons could go forward. Although badly wounded, he refused to be evacuated and went forward with his platoon to the objective giving covering fire during the whole consolidation. The cool, courageous action of Private Munroe enabled his platoon to reach their objective.

In some of the battles Indians painted their faces or shouted traditional war whoops. Early on D Day, Cherokees in war paint were among the first wave of U.S. paratroops in Normandy. Indian passwords and sign language were also used.

In the battle for Normandy, some Canadian Indian members passed several wireless messages in Cree. This totally confounded the Germans who had been listening in. While in training in Britain, an attempt had been made to employ those who spoke Cree as signallers, but the idea was found to be impractical.[8] A similar scheme had been considered and then abandoned in the First World War when it was realized that too many military terms had no Indian equivalent. In World War II, the Navajo in the United States avoided this difficulty by not using translations but their own code of Indian words such as 'fast shooter' to designate a machine gun.[9]

Although it is impossible in this account to delve into all the details of the deaths of all those of native ancestry who were killed, I have selected one particularly poignant account sent to me by D. Charles MacDougall of Antigonish, Nova Scotia.

I first met Sapper Harold Littlecrow early in September 1943 when I was posted to No 2 Platoon, 11th Field Company, Royal Canadian Engineers. At that time the company was stationed in Storrington, south England. It was raining quite heavily as I recall and the men were in their huts awaiting supper call.

I got all my gear together and made my way into No 2 Hut. I had to walk to the far end of the hut before I found an empty bunk. It was an upper. The lower bunk was occupied. The occupant immediately arose to assist me. He introduced himself as Harold Littlecrow. I could tell he was an Indian although he did not resemble the Indians of Nova Scotia. He told me he was from Western Canada. I'll never forget his friendly smile which seemed to go well with his tan-coloured face. The bunk to my right (lower) was occupied by a fellow named Petrie; I never did get his first name. His hair was snow white. He was about 28, which seemed old to me as I was only 18. That evening, Harold, Petrie and I went to supper together.

My first Sunday consisted of the usual spit-and-polish Church Parade. Our platoon was in formation in front of our hut. The platoon sergeant bellowed 'Fall out the RC's!. I was surprised that only three of us fell out —Littlecrow, Petrie and myself. We were on our own when the company marched off. Harold and Petrie guided me through a wooded path which brought us to a small Catholic church where we attended Mass. It was the same every Sunday for us, the three RC's.

Each platoon had four sections of eight men. Harold, Petrie and I were in the same section. Constant training continued until D Day finally arrived. The 3rd Canadian Infantry Division was in the main assault. Our division, the 2nd, was moved to the Folkestone-Dover area.

Our division landed in Normandy on July 7, 1944. The front was about 10 to 12 miles inland near Caen. It took the division two days to land and assemble. We then proceeded to the front. On the way we would stop for a brief rest and then continue on. The closer we got the more shells we encountered. During a short break the platoon rested on the edge of a roadway. A shell land-ed behind us. A piece of shrapnel struck Petrie, killing him instantly. He was our first casualty. The loss of our friend shook Harold and me but we got over it as we moved closer to the front and death was evident all around. The smell of death was like a sickening perfume when moving through those wheat fields.

In late July we were well into the thick of things. The weather was extremely hot and dry, making our chemically treated battle dress very uncomfortable. The objective of the 2nd Division was to sweep down a valley and capture a village. British troops flanked our right which was high, wooded ground. The 3rd Canadian Division flanked our left which was somewhat similar terrain. The British had tough slugging. From the high ground to our right and left we were sitting ducks as mortars peppered the area constantly.

Our section was ordered into the village which was in No Man's Land. We had to check for mines and booby traps. I was selected to drive the section across an open space of about half a mile. It was about 11 a.m. when the section got all the necessary equipment loaded; I then proceeded across the open area. About half-way, shrapnel from a mortar struck my door. It penetrated the door and then went out the window. No one was injured.

We got into the village and unloaded the necessary equipment. The men then got busy checking for booby traps and mines. The village was under German fire but it was not too heavy. The sergeant told the section that we would return for them at about 1400 hours. The sergeant and I then went back to the front which was manned by the Black Watch.

By 2 p.m. enemy fire had increased with great intensity. We could see that the village was being heavily shelled. So was the area separating the front line from the village. We decided, however, to go back and get our section out. We got in the truck and proceeded.

The shelling was unbelievable but we made it into the village with its narrow cobble streets. I stopped near the spot where the section had been let out earlier. Just then our section came rushing out all covered with dirt and plaster. They jumped on the back. I didn't know how I was going to get out as I was facing the Germans. Through the side mirror I could see an alley. I quickly reversed into it with just inches to spare. I then headed back at full speed.

After passing through the Black Watch lines I stopped to let an officer know that we made it. We then drove back some distance and parked in an apple orchard. Everyone started digging in. Harold Littlecrow was digging his trench just behind the tailgate. I had been wearing the same socks for nineteen days and took this moment to change. I was seated on the metal bench of the truck when heavy shelling started again. An 88-mm artillery shell struck the rear of the truck. I don't know if I was blown out of the truck or if I jumped. Anyway, I landed in Harold's slit trench. I was covered in blood. Blood was pouring down my hands and down my legs. I recall seeing two of our men dead (Arsenault and Cooke). I asked Harold if he was O.K. He said 'My stomach hurts a bit, but it isn't much'. He then proceeded to tie bandages to slow the bleeding. I then passed out.

The next thing I knew I was on a stretcher jeep. I faintly remember Harold on a stretcher unconscious beside me. We arrived at a battlefield station and were placed in a field under a scorching sun. I remember an English doctor cutting a hole in my right ankle looking for a vein so I could receive blood. A Scottish padre gave me the last rites. I then fell unconscious.

I never saw my Indian friend again. I learned later that he had died of wounds that day. His stomach wound was worse then he had let on to me. He must have been in great pain when he tended me. He cared for me before he even thought of himself. If I had not received his attention, I would certainly have bled to death. I owe him my life.

But that was Harold's way. Thinking of others but never of himself. Like the people he sprang from, he had a courageous heart and a gentle spirit. His love for life and fellow men beamed all over when he smiled. He had a face that you could read and draw courage from. Part of me was buried with him. I shall always remember him and pray for him.[10]

D. Charles MacDougall

To and Across the Seine

In the course of the German retreat, enemy troops could be encountered anywhere. In one encounter, Private George Leonard Hill of the Essex Scottish was killed not far from Elbeuf, on the Seine River, on August 26. He was a member of the Seneca Tribe of the Six Nations.

Corporal John Robert Spence, a western Ojibway, formerly a member of the Brokenhead Band, Scanterbury, Manitoba, was awarded the Military Medal for an action east of the Seine and some eleven miles north-west of Rouen.

On A 30 August 1944 'B' Squadron, 18th Canadian Armoured Car Regiment (12th Manitoba Dragoons) was carrying out reconnaissance...ahead of the 4th Canadian Armoured Brigade...
Corporal Spence's scout car...the leading vehicle of his troop...was fired on at 150 yards range by a 75-mm anti-tank gun. This gun was one of two anti-tank guns which the enemy was in the process of moving into position in an apparent attempt to stop or delay the advance...Corporal Spence's car ...was disabled. Realizing that the destruction of the enemy guns was essential to prevent them from knocking out two armoured cars and his troop following

closely behind, as well as delaying the armoured regiment of which his troop was the vanguard and notwithstanding the fact that his vehicle...was at point-blank range from the 75-mm gun, Corporal Spence remained with his vehicle and engaged the anti-tank weapons.

The heavy, sustained and accurate fire that he laid down inflicted casualties upon the crew of one gun and drove the remaining members of the gun crew away from the gun,

The investiture of Corporal J.R. Spence by Field-Marshal Montgomery, 16 Dec. 1944. (Public Archives)

thus effectively silencing it. His fire further prevented the crew of the other gun from working it into position from which it could engage our troops and forced the enemy to withdraw in haste.

Corporal Spence's coolness and quick appreciation of the situation and his complete disregard for personal safety under fire were responsible for the prevention of delay in the advance of his troop and of the armoured brigade following closely behind.

The Channel Ports

Advancing rapidly after Falaise, the Allies freed Paris, entered Belgium and moved towards the German frontier. The First Canadian Army had the less glamorous and more difficult job of advancing along the coast. One of its tasks was to help open the Channel ports, the most convenient means of supply for the Allied armies. The clearing of the coast deprived the enemy of the sites for his V-1 flying bombs which had caused loss of life in Britain, disrupted industry and led to the dissipation of the air effort. Rifleman Arthur William Beaver, from the Alderville Band in Ontario, a member of the Queen's Own Rifles, was killed in the coastal fighting.

Battle of the Scheldt

Having broken the backbone of the enemy's resistance near Faliase, Canadian and other Allied troops advanced. They pursued the Germans into Belgium. It was here that the First Canadian Army had perhaps its most important task on the Continent, the clearing of the Scheldt Estuary. Resistance began to increase, particularly at Moerbrugge on the east bank of the Ghent canal near Bruges, where the Germans had brought in strong reinforcements. Corporal Welby Lloyd Patterson, a Six Nations Indian from Ohsweken, earned the Military Medal there.

On the night 9/10 September 1944 'C' Company, Argyll and Sutherland Highlanders of Canada was among other sub-units of the 10th Infantry Brigade which had successfully set a small bridgehead over the canal at Moerbrugge, Belgium. The enemy counterattacked in great strength and acting on his own initiative, Corporal Patterson worked his way through intense enemy mortar and machine gun fire to a position behind two stumps from where for three hours he fired with such coolness and devastating accuracy that the enemy was unable to effectively counter-attack the main position. The courage, initiative and complete disregard for personal safety shown by Corporal Patterson was undoubtedly responsible for the defeat of repeated enemy thrusts at his unit's position.

Corporal Welby Lloyd Patterson

In an action shortly afterwards, Gunner Dick Patrick of the 5th Anti-Tank Regiment's 'A' Troop and a member of the Okanagan Band in British Columbia, accomplished a feat that brought him the MM.

The Argyll and Sutherland Highlanders of Canada and the Lincoln and Welland Regiment secured and for two days held a small bridgehead on the east side of the canal at Moerbrugge during which time a bridge was built. The bridgehead was limited in depth to about 300 yards due to heavy mortar and machine gun fire. Gunner Patrick was a member of a 17-pounder M-10 gun crew which with two tanks of the 29th Canadian Armoured Reconnaissance Regiment crossed the bridge at 0700 hours, 10 September 1944. After the M-10 had shot several suspected enemy positions the actual location of the enemy positions became hard to estimate accurately due to poor visibility and fog. Gunner Patrick asked permission to go ahead on foot and carry out a reconnaissance to locate enemy positions. Despite

the enemy fire he succeeded in getting into the middle of an enemy machine gun position and there opened fire with his light machine gun. His daring attack completely surprised the enemy, who totalled three officers and 52 other ranks into surrender and cleared out a strong point which had pinned the infantry down for approximately two days. The extension of the bridgehead was due in large part to the daring of this gunner.

By the last week of September the great North Sea port of Antwerp was in British hands. Both banks of the long estuary of the Scheldt giving access to the port, however, were still held by the Germans, as was the island of Walcheren. Canadian troops were directed to help clear these areas to permit the use of Antwerp, vital to the advance into Germany. Bitter fighting over open, flooded ground raged throughout October and into early November until the port could be used.

The Rhineland

General Dwight D. Eisenhower, Supreme Commander of the Allied forces, planned to carry the war into Germany on a wide front, beginning in the north. Here the First Canadian Army struck out on February 8, 1945, with the 2nd Division and three British divisions in the initial assault. By nightfall it had smashed the German outpost line. The next obstacle was the Siegfried Line, which ran through the Reichswald, a vast pine forest. To clear the woods and breach the line took five days of fierce fighting. The third and last line of defence before the Rhine ran in front of two wooded areas, the Hochwald and the Balberger Wald; both were in Canadian hands by the night of March 4-5. The Germans fell back across the river on March 10.

The last great obstacle before the Rhine had been a ridge in front of Xanten, crowned along its crest by the Hochwald and the Balberger Wald. It was defended by German paratroopers who had been brought in to bolster the German forces. The 2nd Canadian Corps was ordered to launch an attack on this position. Part of the Corps was the 3rd Infantry Division which included the Queen's Own Rifles of Canada. A member of this battalion was Rifleman Charles Nahwegezhic of the Sheguiandah Band from Manitoulin Island, Ontario. The task assigned to Nahwegezhic's unit was to dislodge the Germans who were firmly entrenched in front of them.

51

On 26 February 1945, number 7 Platoon 'A' Company, 1st Battalion, the Queen's Own Rifles of Canada, attacked a strongly held enemy position over flat open ground...The platoon suffered heavy casualties including the Platoon Commander and Platoon Sergeant. Rifleman Nahwegezhic was seriously wounded in the head but kept advancing. Finally the platoon had to withdraw. Rifleman Nahwegezhic refused to go back and stayed behind with his Bren gun to cover the withdrawal. His accurate and determined fire enabled the balance of his platoon to pull back and reorganize for a further successful attack.

In displaying this supreme courage and devotion to duty Rifleman Nahwegezhic was in large measure responsible for the capture of the platoon objective.

For this action Charles Nahwegezhic, of the Sheguiandah Band from Manitoulin Island, was awarded the Military Medal. The brave warrior died of wounds two days later. His younger brother, Roland, had been killed in action four months earlier in Italy.

On the left flank of the First Canadian Army in late March 1945 in northern Germany was the 3rd Infantry Division. A member of one of its infantry units, the Queen's Own Rifles, was Acting Corporal Harold Jamieson from Ohsweken. In late March and early April, the Queen's Own advanced from the Rhine bridgehead at Emmerich to Hoch Elten, a high wooded ridge near the border with The Netherlands. Here Corporal Harold Jamieson, from Ohsweken, was killed. Shortly afterwards Lieutenant R. Gauthier, his platoon commander, wrote Mrs. Jamieson: "If I had a platoon of men as brave as your son, we could win the war by ourselves. You may well be proud of him."

Not far from the border, Corporal W.L. Patterson, also of Ohsweken, was killed in the taking of Friesoythe on April 14.

Argyll casualties in numbers were light, but of the few who were killed one or two were practically irreplaceable. Corporal Patterson of 'C' Company, who had won the Military Medal at Moerbrugge, was killed by sniper fire...[11]

In April of 1945 the Allied armies advanced into Germany, but much of Holland was still in enemy hands. To open up the country became the First Canadian Army's final task; that of the 2nd Corps was to help clear the northeastern Netherlands.

The Netherlands

By April 1945, the 1st Canadian Corps had arrived in North-West Europe from Italy, had been re-united with the main body of the Canadian field force, and was ready for action. The Corps was assigned to help liberate the western Netherlands.

Private Mike Lavallee in 1942, when he was a member of the Stormont, Dundas and Glengarry Highlanders. (Mrs. Blanche Barrett)

On April 12 Private Norman Joseph Letendre, a Metis member of the Loyal Edmonton Regiment's scouts and snipers platoon, was killed on the Ijssel River. An Indian from Golden Lake, Ontario, Mike Lavallee of the Hasty P's was awarded the Military Medal with the following citation:

On 17 April 1945, the Hastings and Prince Edward Regiment was pursuing the enemy through the densely-wooded country in the area west of Apeldoorn. Private Michael Martin Lavallee was a rifleman in 'B' Company.

As 'B' Company, then the reserve company, emerged from the forest they came under fire from two snipers who had been by-passed by the forward attacking companies.

These two snipers were hidden among the trees on the far side of the clearing. They fired with telling effect and before 'B' Company could take proper cover two other ranks were killed and an officer, a company sergeant major and a signaller were wounded. The situation was particularly difficult because it was impossible to return the fire since some of our own troops were on the opposite side of the snipers.

Realizing that his comrades could not get forward without heavy losses, Private Lavallee on his own intiative decided to engage the two snipers. With utter disregard for his own safety he moved out into the open where he was exposed both to fire from his front and on his flank. Private Lavallee worked his way across the open ground with great skill and singleness of purpose. He skillfully manoeuvred to within 50 yards of the first sniper whom he observed in a tree and brought him crashing to the ground with his first shot. He then deliberately rushed the second sniper firing from the hip as he ran. Taken by surprise by this sudden daring, the second sniper was unable to prevent Lavallee from closing with him and killing him.

The gallant conduct and initiative shown by Private Lavallee is worthy of the greatest praise. As a result of his bravery the reserve company was able to continue to advance without further casualties.

On April 26, American and Russian forces met on the Elbe, cutting Germany in two. Four days later Hitler shot himself. The remaining German forces in Holland surrendered on May 5. The main German surrender took place on May 7, although VE ("Victory in Europe") Day was officially the 8th.

The Canadians suffered more fatal casualties in North-West Europe than in Italy during the Second World War. In North-West Europe the fighting in France exacted the single heaviest toll. This proportion applies as well to fatal casualties of Canadian Indians and Metis.

The McLeods of Wiarton

One Indian family whose sacrifice received much deserved recognition in 1972 was that of Mr. and Mrs. John M. McLeod, Wiarton, Ontario, of the Cape Croker Reserve. John McLeod, a veteran of the First World War, had seen two years of fighting in France. During the Second World War, he enlisted with the Veterans Guard. Two sons were killed overseas: Alfred Joseph, a private in the Perth Regiment, in the Ortona salient on January 17, 1944; and John Joseph, a trooper in the 6th Armoured Regiment south of Caen on July 27. Two more sons, Charles Donald and Malcolm John were wounded in action near Buron, France, on July 8 and two other sons, Max and Reginald, and a daughter, Daisy, also served in the Canadian Army. In 1972 Mrs. Mary McLeod was selected as the Silver Cross Mother of the year and laid the wreath at the National War Memorial in Ottawa.

Mrs. John M. McLeod accompanied by her daughters on the Memorial Chamber of the Peace Tower. (Legion Magazine)

Charlie Byce and Tommy Prince

Charlie Byce

A relatively unknown, quiet and unassuming individual, small in stature but great in courage, who deserves some recognition is Charles Henry Byce, now living at Webbwood near Espanola, Ontario. His mother was an Indian from James Bay, his father, a British veteran, had received the Distinguished Conduct Medal and *Medaille Militaire* (France) in the First World War. On July 4, 1940, Charles Byce enlisted with the Lake Superior Regiment at the age of twenty-three and spent the remainder of the war with this unit. In the later stages of the war Byce became one of the few to win both the Distinguished Conduct Medal and the Military Medal.

During January and February of 1945, many patrols were sent across the Maas River, in The Netherlands.

On the night of 20 January 1945 a fighting patrol of twenty-four all ranks was sent across the River Maas to take prisoners. Corporal

Byce was in charge of a five man section whose job it was to cover the advance of the reconnaissance group. During the advance, the reconnaissance group came under heavy fire from three sides and the success of the patrol was threatened. Cpl Byce, acting on his own initiative, took command of the situation, located the source of the fire as an enemy patrol and drawing forward in the face of point blank fire, he dispersed them with a grenade.

Private Charles H. Byce, age 24, of the Lake Superior Regiment. (Charles H. Byce)

He then came under fire from a camouflaged dugout ten yards to his right and crawling to within a few feet of this position, he threatened the occupant with a grenade and ordered him to surrender. The German fired at him twice, missing him, and Cpl Byce leaped on top of him and took him prisoner. As Cpl Byce was bringing the prisoner out of the trench, he was fired on from another position nearby and the prisoner was killed. Assisted by his platoon commander, Cpl Byce dragged the body out of the line of fire in order to obtain identification from him. At this point several flares went up from the main German position and the party came under heavy fire from Spanduas and mortars. Cpl Byce remained in the face of this fire until he obtained the necessary identifications. As the patrol was withdrawing to their boats, they were attacked by an enemy patrol from the flank with grenades but Cpl Byce advanced on this position, disregarding personal danger, and ordered them to surrender. They continued to fire and Cpl Byce charged them and silenced their fire with a grenade, killing the occupants of the trench, thus allowing the patrol to effect its withdrawal without further casualties. During this whole action, Cpl Byce displayed extreme coolness, courage and devotion to duty. Due to his magnificent efforts the patrol was able to reach its objective and withdraw safely with valuable information. This NCO's aggressive initiative and unselfish gallantry has been an inspiration to all ranks of the unit.

For these actions Corporal Byce was awarded the Military Medal. Some six weeks later, south of the Hochwald Forest, Byce earned the Distinguished Conduct Medal. The citation gives some indication of the exceptional character of this man:

On the morning of 2 March 1945 'C' Coy Lake Superior Regiment was ordered to pass through positions held by 'A' and 'B' Companies in the gap south of the Hochwald Forest. Their objective was a group of buildings. The attack was launched at 0430 hours and by 0600 hours 'C' Company was on its objective. At first light their position became apparent to the enemy and they were immediately subjected to heavy shelling and mortaring. Their three supporting tanks were knocked out and the Company Commander and all the officers became casualties. Acting Sergeant Byce immediately assumed command of his platoon, whose task it was to consolidate the left flank. The enemy were entrenched not more than seventy-five yards away and subjected his platoon to continuous machine gun fire. Sgt Byce realized that his position was untenable as long as the enemy retained possession of their dugouts. He at once organized and personally led an assault on the position and the enemy were driven out after suffering some twenty casualties. By this time the small arms and mortar fire had become most intense. Nevertheless, Sgt Byce continued to move from post to post directing the fire of his men and maintaining contact with the other platoons.

At this time enemy tanks were seen to be manoeuvring into position for an attack. Sgt Byce appreciated that a counter-attack was imminent and, taking the only remaining PIAT, he proceeded to stalk the tanks. His first and second shots at the leading tank missed, thus giving away his position, and the tanks directed their machine gun fire onto him. However, Sgt Byce calmly took aim again and knocked out the tank. As the crew evacuated they were killed to a man by machine gun fire from Sgt Byce's patrol. An enemy tank then appeared at a railway under-pass and Sgt Byce realized that if he could destroy it in the under-pass, this tank would block the others from attacking his position. He then went forward to a house which was a point of vantage but found it occupied by the enemy. Sgt Byce and his single companion cleared the building with hand grenades, but by this time the tank was through and moving onto his position. He issued orders to his platoon to let the tanks, 4 in number, go through them and then to open up on the infantry which was following behind. This they did and the attack was broken up, the enemy infantry withdrawing. The tanks, however, remained commanding the positon

and, with no further anti-tank weapons available, Sgt Byce realized that his platoon was no longer effective. He then proceeded to extricate what remained of 'C' Company. At this phase the enemy called upon Sgt Byce to surrender but he refused and ordered his men back across the bullet swept ground, returning to 'A' Company lines at 1500 hours.

Despite the fact that he had accomplished so much and had fought steadily under the most trying circumstances, Sgt Byce refused to cease fighting. He took up a sniper's position and for the remainder of the afternoon fired at enemy infantry on the railway embankment. He was seen to kill seven and wound eleven. By this action he prevented the infiltration of the enemy into the Company area over ground which was visible only to him in his commanding position. The magnificent courage and fighting spirit displayed by this NCO when faced with almost insuperable odds are beyond all praise. His gallant stand, without adequate weapons and with a bare handful of men against hopeless odds will remain, for all time, an outstanding example to all ranks of the Regiment.

Tommy Prince

In contrast to Charlie Byce who always downplays his bravery was Thomas George Prince. Anxious for fame, Tommy often complained that had he not been an Indian, he would have won the VC (Victoria Cross). He remains perhaps the best known Indian to have worn a Canadian military uniform.

Thomas George Prince was born October 25, 1915, the fifth of eleven children. A member of the Brokenhead Band, Scanterbury, Manitoba, he attended an Indian industrial and agricultural school at Elkhorn where he joined the cadets and proved himself an excellent marksman. He enlisted, in June 1940, in the Royal Canadian Engineers. In September 1942, Prince obtained a transfer to the 1st Canadian Parachute Battalion and a month later was assigned to the Canadian-American First Special Service Force, an elite unit that became known as the Devil's Brigade. On the Anzio beachhead on the Italian west coast, he won the Military Medal.

While in action against the enemy near Littoria, Italy, on 8 February 1944, Sergeant Prince, acting alone, ran a telephone wire from our lines fifteen hundred yards into enemy territory to a house in which he established and maintained an artillery observation post for twenty-four consecutive hours. From his position, Sergeant Prince was not only able to observe enemy artillery emplacements invisible from our lines, but was also directly responsible for the complete destruction by artillery of four such enemy positions which were causing considerable damage to our own troops and material.

At one part of his twenty-four hour watch, Sergeant Prince's communications were cut by shells. Using his own ingenuity, Sergeant Prince donned available civilian clothes and, under direct enemy observation, went out to his line to re-establish contact for target observation.

Sergeant Prince's courage and utter disregard for personal safety were an inspiration to his fellows and a marked credit to his unit.

Prince subsequently landed with the 1st Special Service Force in southern France in August 1944. For gallantry in action near Les Escarene between the 1st and 3rd of September 1944, he was awarded the U.S. Silver Star.

In charge of a two man reconnaissance patrol, Sergeant Prince led it deep into enemy held territory, covering rugged, rocky mountains to gain valuable and definite information of the enemy's outpost positions, gun locations and a bivouac area. So accurate was the report rendered by the patrol that Sergeant Prince's regiment moved forward on 5 September 1944, occupied new heights and successfully wiped out the enemy bivouac area. The keen sense of responsibility and devotion to duty displayed by Sergeant Prince is in keeping with

Among the Canadians decorated...Thomas Prince, front row, right. (Provincial Archives of Manitoba)

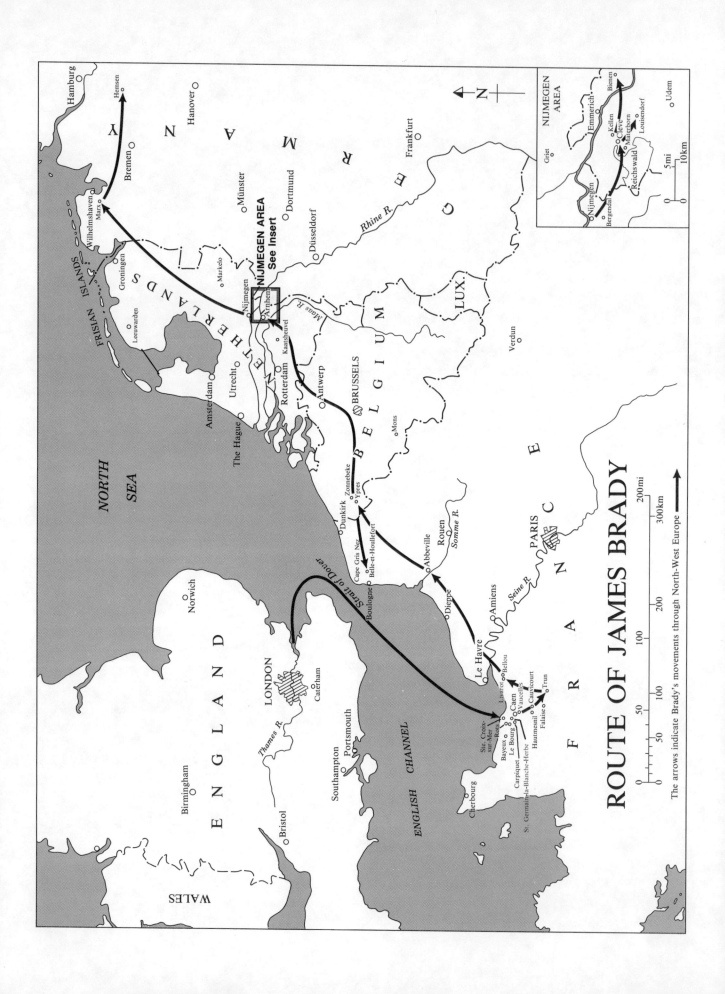

ROUTE OF JAMES BRADY

The arrows indicate Brady's movements through North-West Europe

the highest traditions of the military service and reflects great credit upon himself and the Armed Forces of the Allied Nations.

After the end of the war, Prince returned to civilian life. Five years later, when volunteers were called to join the Canadian Army Special Force for service with the United Nations in Korea, he enlisted in the 2nd Battalion, Princess Patricia's Canadian Light Infantry. After the Korea Armistice Agreement on July 27, 1953, Prince returned to Canada. Owing to further trouble with an arthritic knee, he was unable to serve and was discharged on October 28 of the same year. The post-war years were not easy ones for Tom Prince and on November 25, 1977, he passed away in poverty at age 62.

War Diary of J.P. Brady, Metis

James Brady

James Patrick Brady, a Metis, was born on March 11, 1908, near St. Paul, north-east of Edmonton. He was the second oldest in a family of three boys and five girls. He was an extremely intelligent youngster. His education was mainly at a rural school. When his mother, a nurse, died during the influenza epidemic of 1918, the family broke up. He skipped several grades and in 1922 in high school, Jim received the Governor General's Medal, the highest award a Canadian high school student could receive for academic excellence. As a young man, he worked as a warehouseman and ledger-keeper for a hardware store, but mainly as a farm and seasonal labourer. A leader of the Metis Association of Alberta, he also worked for the communist party and the CCF. He enlisted at Wetaskiwin, Alberta, on June 9, 1943, and underwent training at Brandon, Manitoba. On 22 November 1943, he embarked for Britain. As a signaller in the 50th Battery, 4th Medium Regiment, Royal Canadian Artillery, Jim Brady kept a diary of his experiences in North-West Europe and I have selected excerpts.

Diary

June 16 - July 3
Arrived at Caterham [England] with a party of ten signallers transferred to the 4th Medium Regiment, Royal Canadian Artillery from No. 1 Canadian Artillery Reinforcement Unit.

....The day I joined the unit at Caterham was

marked by the first V-1's falling in southern England. Unit members will remember the monotonous regularity of these explosions when one fell on an average every twenty minutes. June 27th witnessed severe casualties when four men were killed and eight wounded by a near hit on our telephone exchange....

July 6
Embarked on the SS *Fort Brunswick* and stood out in the Thames Estuary where we spent the night awaiting favourable conditions for the Channel crossing.

Gunner James Patrick Brady, Maldegem, Belgium, October 16, 1944. (Glenbow-Alberta Institute)

July 7
Moved out of the Thames Estuary and ran the Dover Straits under the cover of darkness which shielded us from the fire of German coastal batteries at Cape Gris Nez.

July 8
During the night we were bombed but suffered no damage or casualties aboard our craft.

July 9
We disembarked in the late p.m., passed through Ste Croix-sur-Mer [Normandy] and bivouacked to the east of the village.

July 10 - 11

A heavy concentration of refugees from Caen and surrounding districts was seen in all the coastal villages.

July 14

Bastille Day: At Le Bourg [near Caen], we saw a concourse of French villagers singing *La Marseillaise* and listening to a broadcast by General de Gaulle from London.

July 15

In position to the north-east of Rots [north-east of Carpiquet]. During last night our lines were strafed by night bombers. We had no slit trenches owing to the stony ground. Our signal section occupied a low depression or pot hole and we sweated it out.

July 18

We met and talked with some French civilians and were invited in for wine into an estaminet. An old Frenchman with his wife and daughter was excited when we spoke French. He was violently anti-Nazi and tears came as he explained he had lost his father and two brothers at Verdun and his grandfather had been at Sedan in 1870. He bared his breast and showed a mass of wounds. In tears he remarked, "I was also at Verdun in 1916. But during the darkest hours of the occupation I never doubted liberation would come."

July 20

...I visited the monastery of St-Germain-la-Blanche-Herbe which was taken by the Regina Rifles....Apparently the Germans removed all elements among the population they suspected or thought capable of any sabotage or diversion against them in case of invasion. A tactic similar to the removal of our Japanese from the Pacific coast area. The monastery had a huge Red Cross painted on the roof...Inside there was unmistakable evidence the Germans had used it as a tank repair shop as claimed by the French underground.

July 21

Moved before dawn through Caen....A mass grave nearby contained the bodies of 5 French girls shot by the SS.

July 22

At Vaucelles [a suburb of Caen]. Heavy fire directed against enemy tanks—their attack broken up—but we came under intense mortar fire as the enemy have excellent observation points all around the perimeter of high ground which surrounds Caen.

The French underground in Caen executed a French traitor today—a police official who selected and handed over 50 French hostages to the Gestapo.

July 24

Three Canadians were...inexplicably found dead from small arms fire; believed to have been killed by secret civilian snipers or Germans who are still in hiding.

July 25

A welter of rumours about. One that a number of Canadians were shot; some with their hands tied, somewhere near Bayeux. The Chaudieres are alleged to have hanged two French women who lured them into a building. The older French woman and her 14 year old daughter were cohabiting with two German soldiers and these two opened fire when the two Canadians were invited in for a drink of wine. One [Canadian] was killed instantly but the other with his commando knife killed both of the enemy. The French women were hanged to an electric light standard with signal cable.

July 26

A detail of Highland Light Infantry of Canada went through our position to round up enemy reported to be hidden in a sewer....They assisted the French resistance to surround them, but they would not surrender to the French and were all killed. They proved to be four SS men.

July 27

We helped a French woman remove rubble and debris from her estaminet....She was frankly anti-British. This sentiment appears strong in Caen because of the terrific pre-invasion bombings....She considered our troops barbarous and lacking the arts of civilized living.

July 28

A 15-year old Hilter Youth walked over to our observation post and surrendered....He appeared glad to be out of it and laughed as if it was a big joke on Hitler.

August 8

At midnight I stand in our command post and

listen to the thunderous roar of our barrage....
Shortly after midnight the barrage is halted and
we go on call to support infantry....Fire has
been requested by the attacking Scottish infantry....When the Scottish troops advanced they
found a scene of deadly carnage. Not a single
German was found alive.

About 1:30 p.m. I observed US Fortresses approaching from the north-east....Then the front
waves suddenly loosed an avalanche of heavy
block-busters and anti-personnel fragmentation
bombs....Blinding smoke and fumes enveloped

A 5.5-inch gun of the 7th Medium Regiment, R.C.A. in action in
Normandy, August 1944. (Public Archives of Canada)

us. Cries of the wounded could be heard amid
the terrific concussion of the bursting bombs.

When the smoke cleared away and the bombers
passed, the first person I saw was Sergeant E.
Carpenter, Boston, Massachusetts, my immediate superior, almost cut in two by a bomb
fragment. We suffered 19 men killed, 47
wounded, whilst 11 guns and 27 vehicles were
destroyed. A violent day.

August 14
Moved to a position north of Cauvicourt
(Rouvres). About 2:00 p.m. a large force of
RAF and RCAF heavy bombers staged a
daylight raid. Our position was deluged with
bombs. Our unit escaped with the loss of one
killed and four wounded.

On night duty....One of our boys took shelter
in a narrow tunnel. In the darkness he noticed
another occupant. He offered him a cigarette
which was accepted. Upon striking a match he
discovered a German as badly scared as

himself. The German surrendered. He was in
the same orchard as the Polish Ack Ack and
had hidden himself as the Poles have the
unpleasant habit of killing their prisoners occa-
sionally.

August 15
....We seek to block the German army and
close the gap toward Falaise. We have been
issued large yellow silk squares of cloth to iden-
tify our vehicles and ground troops to our aircraft but the enemy have started to use the same
type and colour.

August 16
....The Falaise Gap is now reported to be 6
miles wide and the Nazi escape corridor is
under constant fire.

August 20
Our unit shelled Trun—the narrow exit gap left
to the Nazis....A German general surrendered
after shooting officers who wanted a last ditch
stand.

August 23
Outside Livarot we pass a Hitler *Jugend* in a
green camouflaged sniping jacket blasted by artillery fire....hanging with a death-like grin in a
tree....War is an uncivilized business.

August 24
Paris is said to have fallen yesterday.

August 25
Still resting at Bellou [Normandy]. Seen enemy
wreckage everywhere. Stupendous destruction.
German prisoners were awaiting transport to
the rear....The riversides were literally black
with them.

Later with [Bombardier J.A.] Lemieux we
visited a French family....We were introduced
to their charming daughter, Christiane.
(Lemieux later married her and brought her
back to St-Jerome, Quebec).

August 26
Our forces continue to advance toward the
Seine.

August 27
I talked with a French woman. The SS [had]
whipped her senseless before they left—for no
comprehensible reason except a spirit of pure
sadism....

August 29

Ground soaked. Unable to lie down. Poor shelter. Very uncomfortable.

Sept. 2

We are approaching the region of old British battlefields of World War I and the population seems more spontaneous in their welcome than in Normandy. The Maquis are relentlessly hunting down collaborators. They shot a local French woman who had betrayed two French families who had aided Allied fliers to escape.

Sept. 4

German soldiers are dumbfounded at Allied air might. The Nazis boasted that the Allied invaders would not last as long as the Canadian attackers at Dieppe....We made a night bivouac at Hautmesnil. Here the retreating SS men executed three French police and three civilians including a woman school teacher suspected of being leaders of the local underground. We viewed their bodies behind the church....An RAF bomber crew had been captured by these same SS men. They were hung from trees by their thumbs and shot in their heads.

Sept. 6

We received a tumultuous welcome in the French villages before we reached the Belgian border—hugs and kisses and bands with burning effigies of Hilter in the town square....

Sept. 7

We halted our convoy momentarily in Ypres, and I did traffic control while my boys quaffed a beer at a nearby estaminet....As we entered Zonnebeke I was amazed to watch a sturdy middle-aged Belgian peasant run out of his house and shout in perfect English, "Give it to those goddam Nazi bastards!" Many of the local population can still talk English remembered from the last war.

In Zonnebeke the repentant burgomaster was standing in the street with a halter around his neck and passionately avowing his loyalty and patriotism to Belgium. Two Belgian SS volunteers who had served in Russia were being practically torn to pieces by the mob.

In the p.m. in a nearby orchard we watch the Poles disarm and search 80 German prisoners. A Polish sergeant calmly gut-shot a Gestapo officer whom he recognized disguised in a *Wehrmacht* uniform.

Sept. 9

Hundreds of prisoners still coming in. The Belgians exhibit an excessive zeal in rounding up collaborators. The French were effective but more restrained....I recollect a venerable Frenchman who defined a collaborator as one who had collaborated more than yourself.

Secured a fine billet and slept in a feather bed for the first time since I left Canada.

Sept. 12

We watched the funeral of an entire Belgian family and their friends who had been wiped out by three SS men. A ten-year old girl feigned death although shot through the arm and was the sole survivor.

We went into action in the evening and did some effective shooting.

Sept. 14

Roused up suddenly at 2:00 a.m....Our route led through Ypres and across northern France to Belle-et-Houllefort, a village near Boulogne.

Sept. 15

A French girl walked up to our gun position and brought a large basket of delicious plums. Most of our roughnecks observed she was a luscious plum in herself.

Sept. 20

The die-hard Nazi garrison of 400 men [Boulogne] made a last stand in a bunker. A Canadian officer gave them a 45-minute ultimatum to surrender. It was rejected and we laid down a stonk [heavy barrage] supported by Typhoons and a few heavy bombers. Fourteen men staggered out and finally surrendered.

October 1

Heavy drenching rain has set in ....

November 25

Last day of my leave. In Brussels....whiled away the fleeting hours with an entrancing black-eyed Algerian houri. Alas, back tomorrow to the mud and slaughter again.

November 29

The weather is cold; snow fell today. With [Bombardier R.] Huot I found a billet with a nearby Dutch family. We had difficulty in securing admission. They were badly frightened because the Germans had told them the

Canadians were barbarians, mostly Red Indians, uncivilized, who murdered and scalped on the least provocation. We took pains to be circumspect in every detail and soon got along famously....A small bomb splinter struck me in the left hand. No anesthetic, so mustered up my Indian stoicism and was complimented by the Medical Officer. I told him we have jackfish in our northern lakes who were so big they bite your hand right off. He laughed and I went back on duty.

November 30
At Brakkenstein [a suburb of Nijmegen]. Our battery kitchen is located in a walled-in tennis court. The bedlam of small children begging food at meal time is unnerving. Some of them are so hungry they actually howl like little wolf whelps, while others whine weakly from hunger. We gave away our issues. We could not eat them anyway....

December 5
Hitler Youth reinforcements have arrived in Nijmegen. The Dutch...tell us that these youthful fanatics had the playful custom of patrolling the streets during air raids and throwing live grenades into the cellars of Dutch civilians suspected of having any connection with the pro-Allied underground.

December 22
Stood guard from midnight on. Quite cold.

December 25
The day was notable for its lack of liquid cheer.

December 29
Our unit is withdrawn from static duty.

January 1
A hectic day....Enemy aircraft strafed the front.

January 3
...Huot regaled us with ribald tales of high life and low life, mainly low, in the lower town of Quebec.

January 11
No mail again today. Everyone disgusted.

January 16
Today two Germans came through the 4th Division lines disguised as nuns. They were walking down the street in Kaatsheuvel when

they were recognized and seized by the Dutch police.

February 8
The advance into the Reichswald begins. A heavy barrage at 5 a.m. German strong points, previously registered, are smothered in a tornado of fire....Canadian and British infantry begin to advance....In the first greying dawn I see the tense flushed faces....Already corpses are being brought back, lashed to tops of ambulance jeeps.

At 6:30 a.m. we fire a supporting barrage for the 3rd Canadian Division.

At 11:00 a.m. we fire another barrage as the 2nd Canadian Division goes in with the Maisonneuves leading the assault. The outer Nazi defences have crumbled in a terrible inferno of fire and destruction....Our unit kept up a sustained fire for 13½ hours....Later long lines of prisoners come in. Some reel drunkenly, others stare vacantly, some shamble along in tears, while others laugh hysterically.

February 17
At last we move into Germany....Hundreds of civilian refugees are walking the roads....What a terrific blast of war has passed this way—the utter desolation of these pulverized German towns.

February 22
At Materborn. In action....The German attack began soon after daylight. The infantry got 7 tanks with PIATS and our unit accounted for two in one of the freak shots of the war. While coming out of the woods, apparently an HE (high explosive) went straight down the open hatch of the leading tank. The one advancing nearby parallel to it stopped, caught fire and never moved after that. Two enemy tank men were seen scurrying away in the long growth....

February 23
Went to Cleve and looked over the prison where the Polish slave girls were imprisoned. I will always remember the punishment cells....

February 24
Moved out at daylight to Louisendorf...Was in the middle of a field when we were fired upon by multiple mortars....The blast nearly blew the battle blouse off my back. Suffered shock and difficult breathing. Lay down in the deep

tank tracks and never moved till dark.

February 25

At Louisendorf....Hundreds of Germans are seeking safety behind our lines. I saw a demented old lady straggling along the road wringing her hands—a tragedy of the war...

February 28

We moved into a well-appointed farmhouse and are living on the fat of the land, turkey, beef steak and all the trimmings....We had a real gourmet's feast.

doned our vehicles and took shelter in a basement with a party of Maisonneuves.

March 8

Our forward observation party had a brush with paratroopers. One came up to our gun carrier and surrendered. It was a ruse. He suddenly threw a grendade. [Gunner S.V.] Femia, the crew man, shot him. The remaining number who were in ambush attempted to escape. Some infantrymen came in and the entire enemy group were wiped out.

Blackfriars Bridge, Germany, March 30, 1945. (Public Archives of Canada)

March 1

At Louisendorf. In action....The 2nd Canadian Division moved to attack the Hochwald.

March 4

At Udem....Every foot of the Hochwald is mined—especially with shoe mines—a particularly nasty type of anti-personnel mine which rarely kills outright but usually causes genital wounds when trod upon.

March 5

In action....Civilians are everywhere now. Docile and passive in their behaviour....

March 7

...We were shelled while in convoy....We aban-

March 9

Civilians are everywhere—a problem.

March 13

Moved back to the Maas River in Holland.

March 14

At Vogt. Went and saw the huge German concentration camp where...Dutch people were put to death by the Nazis....

March 17

Our boys had a brawl with the Irish Guards.

March 18

Unit at Bergendal [near Nijmegen]. Resting. A lovely Sunday....

Later I walked with Anna and Nola. Nola is a typical stout Dutch girl. She had a boy friend in the 82nd Airborne Division—a certain Joe X from Massachusetts. There is visible evidence that they did more than hold hands. Nola expects it will be a boy and keeps awaiting the return of her Dear Joe.

March 19
Went after dinner to Nijmegen to see a show, 'The Bandoliers'. Very good, especially the Indian motifs....

March 22
We are back in Germany. We are to support the long expected Rhine crossing.

March 23
At Kellen. An almost continuous action....

March 24
...During the night artillery fire increased all along the front....

At 5:00 p.m. thousands of Allied airborne troops began jumping beyond the Rhine.

April 1
We cross the Rhine at last by Blackfriars [Bailey] Bridge. We went through Bienen. Not a single building remains standing. I saw a stout German Frau weeping while her portly husband sat on the concrete steps of his demolished house. All that remained of their home.

An SS *Panzer* was apparently stalled at a crossroads, under our direct observation, boxed in without hope of escape. They refused to surrender. Our battery knocked them out. I took an SS party book from a dead crew member. The perverted Nazi racial philosophy was grimly revealed in its pages. The document duly recorded all the bearer's ancestors back to the year 1710, attested to his Nordic purity and freedom from any Judaistic taint. (Later I gave this startling booklet to my Jewish friend, Max Weinlos in Edmonton.)

April 12
My 12-day leave came through tonight.

April 25
Rejoined the unit at Griet [11 miles north of Nijmegen]. Was glad to see the boys. Almost like returning to the bosom of your own family.

April 27
In action at Griet. Enemy resistance is weakening all along our front.

May 1
At 10:26 p.m. we heard over the German radio that...Hitler was no more....

May 2
Big news today. The Germans have surrendered in Italy.

May 7
At Marx [12½ miles south-west of Wilhelmshaven]....Here we roust out a German farm family from their house and take it over as our billets.

We converse with a Russian tankist captured at Bialystok in 1941 and a Ukranian peasant girl who were employed as slave labour on the farm. We permit them to use the bedroom of their former master, which gratifies our ironic spirit of revenge.

May 8
At last the wondrous day. Victory in Europe. Our crew, however, are silent and thoughtful ....There is no feeling of exultation, nothing but a quiet satisfaction that the job has been done and we can see Canada again.

We assemble in convoy before noon and await for 'Prepare to move'. Shortly before our departure our new found Russian friend beckons silently and we follow him to the cellar which we had meticulously ransacked yesterday evening without success. Here he indicated to us the secret liquor stock of his former master. What a find! Our troops have a glorious binge.

For a while I retire and remain inert under a hedge....Orientation is a difficult problem but I manage to load our Gun Position Officer into the jeep when the order 'Mount' comes down the line.

May 9
At Hemsen: We assemble and parade before our Officer Commanding, Colonel Gagnon, and march to a memorial service in the little rural church nearby to commemorate those of our regiment who fell in the campaign. The Colonel begins to read the 36 names of our fallen. Tears are in his eyes....

May 13

Five thousand Dutch SS are in cages at Utrecht. In Markelo we see a little Dutch girl almost a child with clipped hair and pregnant—what an aftermath of war, wholesale misery—we witness the sadistic emotions of revenge and it sickens the human spirit...

May 19

Re-attestation circulars for Pacific service distributed. Not many volunteers for Japan. Everyone wants to go home.

Celebrating the liberation of Utrecht, May 1945. (Public Archives of Canada)

May 20

Now doing periodic telephone exchange duty, reports, and unending hours of volleyball.

August 27

1945. [Final entry.]
Laid in a tulip field and rested for an hour under the stars. What beautiful peace and serenity[12]...

James Patrick Brady was repatriated to Canada 9 January 1946 and honourably discharged 11 March 1946 in Calgary. He later worked for mineral exploration companies and on behalf of the Metis. In June 1967 he was lost and died while carrying out mining exploration in the remote Foster Lakes area of northern Saskatchewan.[13]

Indians in Navy and Air Force Blue

In the Second as in the First World War, most Indians served in the infantry. The educational requirements of the RCAF prevented many from joining this branch of the service. When war broke out there was also an air force regulation barring those from commissions who were not of "pure European descent". This was repealed quite early in the war. The Royal Canadian Navy had a more sweeping regulation. Among its prerequisites for service in any rank was a condition that an applicant "be a British born subject, of a White Race". Although it was not

Chief Petty Officer George Jamieson, August 1959. (National Defence)

until February 1943 that this regulation was officially rescinded, a few Canadian Indians and Metis voluntarily joined and were accepted in both services from the outbreak of war. In British Columbia, an unsuccessful attempt was made to obtain a single crew of Indians for the Fishermen's Reserve for patrolling coastal waters.

The story of George Edward Jamieson is similar to that of several other Canadian Indians who joined our navy during the Second World War. His Mohawk father and Cayuga mother had moved from Ohsweken to Toronto. There, George was born and raised and attended school, becoming a member of the Sea Cadets. Being under-age for normal entry into the pre-war Royal Canadian Naval Volunteer Reserve, he was taken on as a boy bugler. He later transferred to the gunnery branch and was in the first lot of reserves called on active service in August 1939. He spent that fall and winter on anti-submarine training. For most of the war he served in escorts on transatlantic and coastal convoy duty, rising to petty officer. He volunteered for the Pacific campaign but the war ended before Canadian forces were sent. George later served on HMCS *Iroquois* during his first tour of duty in Korean waters and remained in the forces until retirement.

Those with Indian ancestry who joined the RCAF could be found in all major theatres scattered among fighter and bomber squadrons. WO 2 (Warrant Officer) Samuel Jeffries from Missanabie, Ontario, was

Sergeant Samuel Jeffries (Royal Canadian Legion, Chapleau)

killed in action December 28, 1942, with No. 104 Squadron RAF harassing Rommel's supply lines. A full-blooded Indian, Flying Officer Richard Robert Chappise, a navigator in the RCAF from Chapleau, Ontario, was killed on June 5, 1945, with No 99 Squadron RAF.

Pilot Officer Willard John Bolduc, whose mother was an Ojibway, from Hearst, Ontario, won the Distinguished Flying Cross with No 15 Squadron RAF of Bomber Command.

In June 1943, while over Cologne his aircraft was attacked by an enemy fighter. This officer's accurate fire damaged the enemy aircraft which broke off the attack and was probably destroyed. Another

time during a sortie against Nuremberg his aircraft was attacked by a Junkers 88. While making the bombing run Pilot Officer Bolduc opened fire and the enemy fighter fell to the ground in flames. At all times this air gunner has set an inspiring example by his keenness and devotion to duty.

He died in June 1968 and was buried in Chapleau.

A good number of Mohawks from the Bay of Quinte area, probably due to their familiarity with military aircraft on and near their reserve, joined the RCAF. One of them, Charles Clinton Topping, joined the RCAF and was sent overseas eventually becoming a member of No 226 Squadron RAF. In the summer of 1941, Sergeant Topping, age 22, was lost on a bombing mission.

For many who served, the war was a time of danger and adventure, an opportunity to travel and escape the confines of home and family. Some look back on it as the happiest time of their lives. Canadians found themselves in parts of the world that they would never likely have had the occasion to visit in civilian life. Young men, such as Albert R. Corston, of Scottish and Cree ancestry, from Chapleau, nicknamed 'the Chief', joined the RCAF during the Second World War. He took his initial elementary flying training at Goderich, Ontario, on Fleet Finches and at Aylmer, Ontario, on Harvards. Posted overseas, he arrived in England on August 17, 1942.

After some additional training and flying experience, he was issued with tropical kit and embarked from Liverpool with his buddies. The convoy moved slowly along the west coast of Africa. A U-boat attack near Freetown made the 110° on the troopship seem even hotter. Eventually, however, he reached Bombay, India, and ended up with No. 67 Squadron RAF. Many places that he had only learned about in geography in school, he was now able to see.

When the Japanese attacked Calcutta on 5 December 1943, Al Corston was nearby to help defend the city. When the alarm was sounded, his squadron was scrambled. In the air battle, Al's Hurricane was hit in the radiator by a Japanese Zero and put out of action. After a bumpy but safe landing in a rice paddy, he was surrounded by curious local inhabitants and taken to the nearest village. He gave a friendly greeting to two officers in the Indian Army, whereupon both quickly drew their revolvers. His non-British accent and appearance made them suspect that he was Japanese. However, he convinced them he was an "Indian" ally.

Shortly after his return to base, a reporter from the *Daily Mirror* interviewed Al. The reporter was in this theatre in an attempt to give more press coverage to this less known area of the war. It was thought that the story of a Canadian Indian in the RAF might be of interest to the British public. After the war, Al learned of the content of the story from an aunt who had seen his story reproduced in the *Sudbury Daily Star*. It seems that the reporter had perpetuated the British public's general impression of North American Indians derived from Hollywood movies and popular fiction. The article gave the impression that Al came from an area in Canada where the 'natives' were still in "loincloths and feathers, lurking in the shadows ready to massacre white people."

After additional service as an instructor, Al returned home following the end of hostilities, fell in love and married "the girl next door". Happily married for over thirty-five years, Mr. and Mrs. Corston and family now reside in Toronto, Ontario.[14]

Heraldry

This country's native people have a proud history as brave warriors. Often they were reluctant to go on the warpath, yet when they took up arms, they proved to be formidable fighters. Their military service to this country in both World Wars, previously unrecognized, is shown to be also distinguished.

Heraldic Crest, No. 421 Squadron (Canadian Forces Photo Unit)

The very name of this country is derived from the Iroquois word *Canada* (gana:da) meaning community or village. Similarly, a great many other aspects of native culture have been adopted and have become part of the fabric of this country. Thus, in time of war, it is not surprising that the legendary fighting qualities of our native people are reflected in military heraldry. This was evinced in the naming of air squadrons and ships during the Second World War as well as after. The badges of Nos. 421, 422 and 431 RCAF Squadrons pay tribute to the Canadian Indian. Tribal Class destroyers such as *Athabaskan, Haida, Huron, Iroquois, Micmac, Nootka,* as well as

Heraldic Crest, Algonquin Regiment (C.F.P Unit)

other vessels of the Royal Canadian Navy have Indian names with accompanying appropriate badges. Also one unit of the Canadian army, the Algonquin Regiment, bears the motto NE-KAH-NE-TAH, (We Lead, Others Follow).[15] Based on my research in both World Wars the fighting qualities of Canada's Indians typified in heraldry of the Canadian forces is well founded.

Conscription

On June 21, 1940, after the defeat of France, the Canadian Parliament passed the National Resources Mobilization Act (NRMA). Although service overseas remained voluntary, conscription for service in Canada was now the law of the land and young men were required to report for thirty days' military training. The period of training was extended in February 1941 to four months and NRMA men were subsequently required to serve for the duration of the war in the Western Hemisphere. To implement conscription for home defence there had to be national registration. Between August 19 and 21 all men and women who had reached the age of sixteen were required to register. The information thus obtained was used not only for compulsory military service but also to direct and control civilian labour.

Indians were to register through the Indian Agent on each reserve. One copy of the registration form of single Indian men between 19 and 45 was sent to the National War Services Division and those eligible were subsequently called up for military training and home defence service. The Department of Justice ruled that Indians could not be excused from this form of military service. Although Indians were exempted in the First World War, the government maintained that the nature of conscription in the Second World War was different. Conscription in the 1914-1918 war had provided for continuous service overseas whereas the 1941 law required only training and service in Canada. By April 1942 it had become apparent that the enforcement of this law on Indians, especially in remote areas, was difficult. Many were found to have some physical infirmity and the time and expense required in their apprehension was wasted.[16] Inuit were not to be subject to compulsory military service.[17] As a result of this policy of registration, however, some who considered themselves Indians, usually of mixed blood, but did not have treaty status, were put off reserves.

As the war proceeded, pressure for a policy of general conscription for service anywhere gradually increased. In January 1942 it was announced that a national plebiscite was to be held on April 27 asking voters to release the government from its earlier pledge not to extend conscription to overseas service. The results showed that a majority of Canadians, almost 65 per cent, had voted to release the government from its past promises. In Quebec, however, a substantial majority, about 75 per cent, rejected the proposal, insisting that pledges should be kept. A clause in the National Resources Mobilization Act was amended permitting the employment of conscripts overseas by Order-in-Council. Then Mackenzie King's policy was expressed in the phrase "not necessarily conscription but conscription if necessary."

Among the treaty Indian population, particularly on Caughnawaga[18] and Ohsweken, there was some opposition to overseas conscription. Considering themselves a separate national entity, the Six Nations refused to admit that these laws applied to them.

From mid-1943, with the assignment of part of the Canadian Army to operations in Italy, casualties increased significantly and had to be replaced. With the commitment of the remaining overseas divisions to France in the summer of 1944 the demand for reinforcements further increased. The prolongation of the war into a winter campaign brought the whole infantry reinforcement problem to a crisis. Since volunteers were not forthcoming in sufficient numbers, the use of those conscripted for home defence under the NRMA, the so-called "zombies", appeared to be the answer. In November 1944 it was decided that conscripts were to be sent overseas. There were protests in Quebec and a brief mutiny among some troops stationed in British Columbia.

The question of compulsory military service for Indians was discussed by Cabinet in December 1944. It was confirmed by the government that all Indians were to be liable for military service. However, certain tribes that had signed Treaties 3, 6, 8, and 11, were to be exempt only from compulsory military service overseas.[19] The minister responsible for the Indian Affairs' Branch, T.A. Crerar, was a member of the Cabinet strongly in favor of overseas service for conscripts. Although the Indian community of Canada was behind the war effort, to those who did not have full Canadian citizenship, it seemed unjust that they should be compelled to serve overseas.

Indians in Treaties 3, 6, 8, and 11 Exempted from Overseas Conscription

"TREATY No. 3

Agencies
Fort Frances
Kenora
Port Arthur
Sioux Lookout

TREATY No. 6

Agencies
Rocky Mountain House
Saddle Lake
Battleford
Carlton
Duck Lake
Onion Lake
Edmonton
Hobbema

TREATY No. 8

Agencies
Athabasca
Fort St. John
Lesser Slave Lake

TREATY No. 11

Agencies
Fort Norman
Fort Simpson
Fort Resolution"[20]

The Home Front

By late 1941 rapid industrialization for the war effort had created an enormous demand for labour. It was necessary to train workers in both vocational schools and on the job in order to teach skills that had never previously been required in Canada. Competition for manpower developed between the greatly expanded armed forces and industry. To alleviate the manpower shortage the government adopted measures to encourage women to join the labour force. Indians benefitted but only marginally as some did receive new training.

Socially, the war had a significant effect. The absence of a husband often weakened family life but usually improved income. The dependent's allowance for a wife and children or mother gave many Indian families increased incomes. Many who had been living on reserves moved to cities where there were better job opportunities. In keeping with the trend of the shift of the rest of the Canadian population from the country to the town and cities, there was a movement of Indian and Metis people to urban areas of Canada during the war.

On the west coast, there was fear of a Japanese invasion following the attack on Pearl Harbor. The occupation of the Aleutian Islands of Attu and Kiska by the Japanese in June 1942 created further alarm. The firing of a few shells by a Japanese submarine at Estevan Point on Vancouver Island, witnessed by Indians on a nearby reserve,[21] prompted civil defence measures in British Columbia, including Indian reserves along the coast.[22]

On the Pacific coast, the Rocky Mountain Rangers at one point had about two companies of Indians. This battalion formed part of the force that landed on Kiska in August 1943 only to find that the Japanese had already left.

Another unit on the west coast that attracted a good number of Indians from British Columbia was the Pacific Coast Militia Rangers. This group was raised in February 1941 in response to fear of possible Japanese attacks. Fishermen, trappers, farmers and other residents of the coastal region were recruited to help patrol the coast, stop sabotage or minor enemy incursions and provide information for the regular forces.

The opening up of Canada's north also brought the native people there increased contact with the white man. New projects in Canada's north, largely American, included a highway from Dawson Creek, British Columbia, to Fairbanks, Alaska, with an accompanying oil pipeline from Norman Wells, Northwest Territories, to Whitehorse in the Yukon as well as aircraft ferrying facilities. In Labrador, Goose Bay airport was built and became an important air

link to Iceland and Scotland. The number of weather stations in remote areas was also increased to improve weather forecasting. The establishment and expansion of military bases for training, including the British Commonwealth Air Training Plan, brought large numbers of servicemen into close contact with Indian settlements.

Also during the war, rationing was introduced in 1942. Gasoline, sugar, coffee, tea, butter, meat, preserves and evaporated milk were rationed and ration books were issued for everyone. For those living in remote areas, larger amounts could be purchased at one time.

Gideon Eneas (1892-1955), hereditary chief of the Penticton Band, a member of the 71st Company Pacific Coast Militia Rangers. (R.N. Atkinson Museum, Penticton)

Indians were generous in contributing to war charities. The Red Cross was a favourite recipient of donations.[23] Indian bands and individuals bought war bonds and war savings certificates. Chief Peter Moses of the Old Crow Band in the Yukon was particularly active in raising funds for the war effort and was awarded the British Empire Medal for his efforts.

The Blackfoot Band on the Bow River, in Alberta, made a remarkable effort in collecting scrap. They salvaged scrap metal, old tires and over 125 tons of buffalo bones. They also collected money to assist British war orphans.[24]

The enlistment of men in the armed forces, coupled with the needs of war industries, resulted in a shortage of loggers. As a result, some Indians found work in forestry. Those engaged in farming and fishing profited from higher prices and increased demand. Members of a number of Indian bands located along the border entered the United States to work. Some were drafted. If medically fit, the only way they could be excused was to transfer to the Canadian forces for active service overseas.[25]

By 1942-43 the financial lot of Indians on the home front was generally improving, as is evident from the excerpt of this report of the Inspector of Indian Agencies for Alberta:

> Work has been very easy to find, with farmers and ranchers, stooking and threshing; also working in beet fields, in logging camps, lumber mills, airport construction work, railroad section crews...A number

Chief Peter Moses wearing his medal poses with his wife and grandson in front of their cabin, Old Crow, Yukon. (Yukon Archives)

> work on the new highway to Alaska; others act as guides and river pilots for the American Army passing through the northern part of the Province and Northwest Territories; some of these earn from $8.00 to $12.00 per day. Unfortunately, all this affluence has had its deleterious effect, more so with these northern Indians; intoxication and gambling increased....[26]

Before the war was over, various studies were undertaken to help in post-war planning. In Britain, Sir William Beveridge released a report advocating reforms aimed at achieving a post-war welfare state. In Canada a similar study proposed government spending to prevent post-war depression. To meet the electorate's demand for social reform and increased social security, Mackenzie King charted a moderate course. In 1944 came the Family Allowances Act—a monthly "baby bonus" for each child under sixteen. It helped to supplement family incomes including those of native families.

The Second World War helped end the isolation of many native people from the white community. As a result of their participation in the war and the general impulse for social reform there was renewed interest in improving their conditions. Some changes were effected but they were only a small step in the direction of full advancement.

During the First World War native women helped in war effort by working in voluntary organizations that raised money and provided medical supplies and comforts for the troops. The Second World War also afforded native women the opportunity to serve in voluntary organizations as well as industry and as non-combatants in the women's branches of the forces.

Among those who joined the forces was Marguerite Marie St. Germain, now Mrs. Philip Plante, a Metis from the Peace River valley of Alberta. In 1942 Marguerite, age 20, enlisted in the RCAF Women's Division. Leading Airwoman St. Germain ended up for a good part of the war at No. 3 Flying

"A.W. 1 Margaret Pictou" by F/Sgt. D.Y. McMillan. (Margaret LaBillois)

Instructor School at Arnprior. She recalled that while early in the war Metis were insulted with names such as 'skunk hunter', prejudice diminished as the war progressed and the Metis proved they could perform as well as anyone else.

Another who joined the Women's Division of the RCAF was Margaret LaBillois (nee Pictou), born in the 1920's on the Eel River Reserve, Darlington, New Brunswick. She was the second eldest of five children, and her ambition was to become a nurse. As her parents were separated and the family was dependent on their mother for financial support, Margaret decided to forego nursing training following graduation from high school and instead, to go to work. As most of the eligible men on the reserve had enlisted, including her two brothers and a boyfriend (whom she married after the war), Margaret enlisted in the Women's Division of the RCAF. To help support her family, she sent home half of each month's pay.

Most of her time of service was spent in the photographic unit at Rockcliffe. She found her service there a positive experience and did not encounter any discrimination. The saddest part of the war for her was the loss of her adopted brother, L/Cpl Matthew Bernard. "For years I could not talk about him

Mrs. Margaret Paudash and her two sons, Elmer (left) and George Jr. (right). (Mrs. June Robinson)

without tears." At present, Margaret lives on the same reserve, the proud mother of six boys and six girls and twelve grandchildren. Anxious to preserve her Indian heritage, she now teaches the Mic Mac language at the local school and is an active member of the Union of New Brunswick Indians.

Dependents' Allowance

When treaty Indians with dependents enlisted at the outbreak of war, their families received the same allowance as other servicemen. In 1941-42 new procedures and methods were developed for Indian dependents. It was claimed that treaty Indians were receiving too much money and were unable to manage it properly; thus in early 1942 some allowances were placed under the control of the local Indian Agent. As well, Indian servicemen and their dependents were strongly urged to invest some of the allowance in war savings certificates or in the Indian trust fund at Ottawa if they wished to receive the maximum benefit. Although there were some cases of financial mismanagement by wives, most had been quite responsible in handling their allowances.[27]

The formal education of the Indian varied in quality but was usually poor. During the war the shortage of qualified teachers was even more pronounced in Indian schools. Some teachers joined the armed forces, others took more lucrative jobs in war industries. Students were forced to take correspondence courses. Pupils were often just supervised in the schools and their work sent out for correction.[28]

To mark an Indian soldier's departure, death or safe arrival from overseas, Indian communities carried out Christian and even traditional ceremonies. There were get-togethers and farewell dances in honour of those leaving for overseas. During the Second World War some of the young Indian recruits from the Prairie Provinces who were going overseas approached veterans of the Great War who seemed to have been protected by the spirits for their advice and blessing. For the fallen a Christian memorial service or even traditional dance was held. Victory dances were sometimes held for those who came back and thanksgiving offered for their safe return. At the time of the First World War these dances had been discouraged; certain others, such as the Sun Dance, had even been forbidden.

To give an assessment of prejudice in the Canadian forces and in Canadian society against native people is not simple. I have shown evidence of some official discrimination in the forces. Yet perhaps even more sinister is prejudice and bigotry encountered on a personal level. It appears to have been relatively worse for those Indians serving in Canada rather than those overseas. It became especially difficult, however, for some British war brides. One such example was Mrs. George Paudash.

The Paudash family of the Hiawatha Band, on the north shore of Rice lake near Peterborough, Ontario, has a notable record in both wars. Brothers George and John (1875-1959) (see page 20) Paudash George cellent snipers with the 21st Battalion in the First World War. Two of George's sons, George Jr. and Elmer, enlisted in the Second. Elmer was killed in September 1942 while on a bombing mission over Germany; George Jr. served in North-West Europe with the Stormont, Dundas and Glengarry Highlanders. While in England he met and married Anne Rosemary Hacker from Bognor Regis in Sussex. Mrs. Paudash encountered prejudice in Canada and spoke out in an interview in 1951:

> Most Canadians, I've found, are as confused about Indians as I was before I married one, and many look down on the whole race....The reputation of Indians for their lack of chivalry toward women is about as silly as the notion that they still live in wigwams....As far as the traditional 'silent Indian' is concerned, I think between my husband and the average Englishman, my husband is the more talkative....[29]

By marrying an Indian, she became one herself according to the Indian Act. Upon acquiring that status, she found the laws then in effect prohibiting treaty Indians from voting or from being served liquor discriminatory. In dealing with the Department of Indian Affairs she encountered "red tape as thick as war paint". In contrast to the white community, the Indian people made her feel at ease. She remembers while in hospital, after giving birth, a woman in the bed next to her asked where she was from. When I told her "Hiawatha", she replied, "a lot of those Indians are pretty dirty aren't they?" Mrs. Paudash angrily told her that "any Indians I know are just as clean or cleaner than anyone else".[30]

Mr. George Paudash died in December 1982 bringing to an end a wonderful marriage of over thirty-five years. Mrs. Paudash remembers her husband as "thoughtful, considerate, a good father and a good husband."[31]

Although the extent of the problem has been exaggerated, one of the adjustments some treaty Indians faced in the forces, particularly in the Second World War, was the general availability of alcohol overseas. The law as it applied to treaty Indians and

alcohol, i.e. the illegality of selling intoxicants to Indians, in Canada, brought about after the Second World War the formation of several all-Indian Legion branches on reserves, where alcohol was permitted if so voted in a referendum by the particular reserve.

Veterans' Benefits

Prior to the outbreak of the Second World War, those now responsible for Indian Affairs recognized that their predecessors had erred in allowing much reserve land to be sold for Soldier Settlement at the end of and just after the First World War.[32] Thus when formal requests came in 1944, the answer was different. In response to the St. Paul Branch (No 100) Canadian Legion, that land of the Saddle Lake Agency be opened up for settlement by veterans as it was not being cultivated, Thomas A. Crerar, the Minister of Mines and Resources, who was responsible for Indian matters replied:

> After the last war this group of Indians consented to release for white settlement a block of land consisting of 18,720 acres all of which is now in white occupation. It is quite possible that in this instance the Indians were generous to their own detriment. The problem of providing means of livelihood and occupation will carry us far into the future and the provision for them, wisely made in the Treaty of 1876, may not now be denied them. Their remaining lands are not considered to be any more than sufficient for the ultimate requirements of the Indians who incidentally are making some progress in agricultural pursuits. That it has not been more rapid is a matter of regret to this administration but the process of transition from hunting and trapping to agriculture is a slow and arduous one.
>
> Any further surrender of Indian lands suitable for agricultural purposes would in the judgement of this office be unwise and would not be regarded with approval by the Indian administration.[33]

Most Indian bands themselves now were generally opposed to selling any of their agricultural land for settlement by veterans although some reserve land was acquired by the Veterans' Land Administration.

Certain benefits were established by the Department of Veterans Affairs to assist returned service personnel. Among the beneficial programmes was the Veteran's Land Act (whose provisions also applied to commercial fishermen). This Act was much more helpful to Indians than the land settlement scheme of the First World War. Up to $2,320 could be granted to an Indian veteran who settled on Indian reserve land.[34] Any veteran settling on Crown land received this same grant. Up to $6,000 in loans was available to veterans, including Indians, who wished to settle on private farm land. If all payments were made, the government would absorb an amount up to $2,320. Approximately 1,800 Indian veterans were established on Indian reserve land under the provision of *The Veteran's Land Act* before the final deadline for qualified veterans to apply was reached.[35] There were as well those Indian veterans who settled off the reserves. Among the benefits available to all veterans were money for university education as well as vocational and technical training and re-establishment credit for home-building or to set up a business.

After the First World War many Indian veterans who settled on reserve land to farm, and were granted occupancy rights, had been unable to repay their loans owing to a variety of circumstances. Their land, however, could not be seized and sold to white farmers in order to compensate for any financial loss, as the land was part of a reserve. The land could only be acquired for use by another treaty Indian.

For qualified Indian veterans of the Second World War who wished to farm on the reserve, an outright grant of $2,320 was made. Unlike other veterans settling off the reserve, the Indian veteran could not pledge reserve land as security in the event of a loan default. This was part of the reasoning for a grant rather than a loan. There has been some controversy as to whether the grant of $2,320 was discriminatory or not. From the evidence I have found, I do not think it was.

Some Canadian Indians living close to or on the border with the United States enlisted in the American forces during both wars. During the Second World War, there is a record of over seventy who elected to receive benefits under Canada's Veterans' Land Act. Most were from Caughnawaga, St. Regis, the Six Nations (Ohsweken) and Walpole Island. Among some of their reasons for joining the American forces were more lenient physical standards, better pay and less discrimination. Canadian Indians serving in the American forces who moved to the United States were eligible for American veterans' benefits. In the United States, no special provisions were made for the treaty Indian veteran, especially

for those wishing to farm on a reserve; they had to obtain a loan.[36] In contrast to his Canadian counterpart who was entitled to a non-repayable grant of $2,320 if he settled on a reserve, the American Indian veteran often needed the assistance of band funds as loan security, since treaty land could not be mortgaged.[37]

The Emergence of Veterans as Native Leaders

One of the common positive aspects of native people, including Canadian Indians, in the Allied forces was the friendships that developed. The cohesive force, for example, of a rifle platoon fighting together against the enemy overcame any previous racial feelings. Another interesting aspect of the military participation was the emergence of native leaders with service backgrounds.

As in the First World War, treaty Indian veterans of the Second World War were given the right to vote in federal elections if they so desired without losing their treaty status. Some Indian veterans of both wars gained an increased awareness of their identity. Some sought to help their people by setting up their own organizations to lobby for reform and to protect existing native rights.

Some of those who had served in the forces emerged with new confidence in their own ability. Some gave expression to this feeling in a greater desire to organize and lead their people. One Great War example of an Indian rights activist was Frederick Ogilvie Loft who had been born on the Six Nations Reserve at Grand River in 1862. Loft had served in France with Canadian railway construction troops and in Britain with the Canadian Forestry Corps. In September 1919, he formed an organization known as the League of Indians of Canada. The League faltered during the Great Depression, partly as a result of bureaucratic opposition. (Loft's story can be found in *John Tootoosis: A Biography* by Norma Sluman and Jean Goodwill, 1982.) From the Second World War emerged many others, such as Walter Deiter, OC (Order of Canada), of the Federation of Saskatchewan Indians and the National Indian Brotherhood, (now the Assembly of First Nations), also former president of the National Indian Veterans Association. The late Omer Peters, from the Moraviantown Reserve, who was with the RCAF, served his band as chief, councillor and administrator prior to helping organize the Union of Ontario Indians. Peters eventually became vice-president of the National Indian Brotherhood.[38] One of the many Indians who served in the Royal Canadian Artillery was Charles Paul now with the Union of New Brunswick Indians. Another veteran, Melville Hill, worked on behalf of the Mohawks of the Bay of Quinte.

Several prominent Metis leaders saw military service during the Second World War. Malcolm F. Norris (1900-1967), who joined the air force, helped organize the Metis and Indians of Alberta and Saskatchewan. James Patrick Brady (1908-1967), a gunner in the Royal Canadian Artillery, had worked with Norris to found and organize the Metis Association of Alberta.[39] Joe Amyotte, born in 1913, served in the Canadian army, becoming the first president of the newly formed Metis Society of Saskatchewan in 1967. Dr. Adam Cuthand, also

Corporal Malcolm Norris and his son, Leading Aircraftman Arnold Willy (right), Camrose, Alberta, 1942. (Murray Dobbin)

born in 1913[40] and a wartime member of the Canadian army, rose to become founding president of the Manitoba Metis Federation in 1968.[41]

Not a few of Indian ancestry have enjoyed success and made a substantial contribution to this country. It is impossible to name them all since many Canadians from all segments of our society have varying amounts of Indian blood.[42] One example, a veteran, is Arnold William Norris whose father,

Malcom F. Norris, was mentioned earlier. While his younger brother enlisted in the Canadian army, Willy joined the air force hoping to become a pilot. There was a surplus of pilots so he ended up as a navigator with No. 433 Squadron. During a raid on Dusseldorf, April 22/23, 1944, his Halifax was shot down by a German fighter over northern Belgium. He was the only member of the crew to survive. His brother was not as fortunate. Private Russell John Norris of the North Nova Scotia Highlanders, age 20, was killed by a mortar shell at Tilly-la-Campagne, Normandy on July 25, 1944. Following over a year as a POW in Germany, Willy Norris returned to Canada in mid-July of 1945. He attended university, with the help of veterans' benefits, receiving a Ph.D. in geology from the University of Toronto. At present, he is with the Geological Survey of Canada at Calgary where he resides with his wife and family.

Willy Norris recalls a meeting prior to D Day, with his brother in England. At the time, Russell John foretold that Willy would survive and he would be killed. The strength of belief in one's premonitions and dreams vary among societies and individuals. In traditional Indian culture, dreams have great significance. For example, on a war party, a brave could be allowed to withdraw if moved to do so by an unfavourable dream. This would not be considered an act of cowardice, though in our society it would.

Another Metis veteran with a notable career is Roger Teillet. His Metis ancestry originates from his maternal grandfather, who was Louis Riel's brother. Roger was born in St. Vital, Manitoba, on August 21, 1912. He was educated in St. Vital and at St. Boniface College. Fluent in English and French, he acquired only a few words of Cree. From 1935 to 1940, he was with a life assurance and annuity company in St. Boniface. He married Jeanne Boux of St. Boniface in May 1940. Roger enlisted in October 1940 with the RCAF. Upon completion of his training as an observer, he was commissioned. He was sent overseas in September 1941. On his twenty-fourth operational trip, Flight Lieutenant Teillet was shot down and taken prisoner. Following liberation and return to Canada he left the RCAF to re-enter the insurance business, eventually purchasing his own agency in 1950.

Roger became interested in politics, and from 1953 to 1959 served as the representative for St. Boniface in the Legislative Assembly of Manitoba. He was first elected to the House of Commons in 1962. From 1963 to 1968, he was Minister of Veterans Affairs. Following his retirement from politics, he served as a member of the Canadian Pension Commission for eleven years. Happily retired, he now resides in Ottawa.

PART IV

A Comparison with Native Peoples in Australia, New Zealand and the United States

In order to better view the effort of Canada's Indians in both World Wars, it is appropriate to compare their contribution and treatment with the native peoples of other Allied countries. It is possible from existing evidence to detect similarities and differences with Australia, New Zealand and the United States. Aboriginal contributions during the wars should be viewed, however, in the context of their past history, particularly relations with white government and society.

Australia

During the First World War, while the percentage of fatal casualties among Australian aborigines was higher, proportionately more Canadian Indians enlisted. As well, it should be noted that overall Australian casualties were also higher than Canadian.[1] Just under three hundred aborigines from New South Wales, Queensland and Victoria, enlisted in the Australian Imperial Force.[2] Of these, forty-four were killed or died of wounds.

Several Aborigines were decorated but not as highly as some Canadian Indians. It was not until the

Reg Saunders receives his commission, Seymour, Victoria, Australia, November 25, 1944.

Second World War that an aborigine, Reg Saunders, was commissioned in the Australian Army. In this regard, the Canadian record is much better in both World Wars.

The Australians had a few defence units comprised largely of aboriginals below the rank of sergeant such as the Torres Strait Defence Force and the Northern Territory Special Reconnaissance Unit.[4] Their pay scales were less than those of white soldiers, which resulted in mutiny in January 1944. A raise was granted but the level of pay was still below the amount received by white soldiers. There was no such discrimination in pay based on racial background in the Canadian Army.

The Australian Army in the Northern Territory proved a good employer of civilian Aborigines. As well as paying them, it supplied training such as basic auto mechanics, good rations and adequate housing as well as free hospitalization and clothing for the Aborigine and his dependents. Some problems arose such as culture shock or of white servicemen and workers in Canada and elsewhere.

During the war, an invaluable lesson learned was the desirability of "raising the self esteem of the Aborigines as a contribution toward the raising of their racial morale."[5] Had this lesson been vigorously followed earlier in Canada's past relations with its Indians, their lot might have been better.

New Zealand

The Maoris of New Zealand have an outstanding war record. During the First World War, of a total Maori population of about 50,000, some 3,000 enlisted. Between February 1915 and October 1918, a total of 2,227 Maoris went overseas. They served as infantry in Gallipoli and in a pioneer battalion in France and Belgium. Total casualties were almost fifty per cent, 336 being fatal. Members of the Maori pioneer battalion received three Distinguished Service Orders, four Distinguished Conduct Medals, nine Military Crosses and thirty-eight Military Medals.[6]

During the Second World War permission was given to form a separate Maori infantry battalion. The Maori population was then about 100,000. About 16,000 saw service and of these some 7,000 were in the battalion. It suffered approximately 2,600 casualties, of which 640 were fatal.[7]

Key positions in the battalion were at first held by specially selected new Zealanders of European ancestry. However, as the war progressed, Maoris increasingly filled these positions. In fact, of a total of ten commanding officers, six were Maoris.[8]

Many Maoris were decorated in the Second World War. Among the awards for bravery for their bat-

force and at sea. As there was no New Zealand Navy, those wanting a naval career joined the Royal Navy. A colour bar prevented Maoris receiving naval commissions. Some were commissioned in the navy and air force during the Second World War but no official record is available.

How were Maori returned servicemen treated, one might ask? I have found no differentiation between veterans of European or Maori ancestry as far as pensions are concerned. It does appear, however, that Maori veterans of the First World War were not eligible for full rehabilitation assistance. The Australian, Canadian, New Zealand and American public were

Members of the Maori Battalion in Italy open their Christmas parcels, 1944. (Alexander Turnbull Library)

talion were one Victoria Cross, seven Distinguished Service Orders, thirteen Distinguished Conduct Medals, twenty-four Military Crosses and fifty-one Military Medals.[9] The VC winner was Second Lieutenant Te Moana-nui-a-Kiwa Ngarimu. He earned the Commonwealth's highest award south-west of El Hamma, Tunisia.

In the First World War, Maoris served in the air

generally opposed to any preferential programmes for native veterans at that time.

The distinguished record in the Second World War of the Maori battalion helped remove any vestiges of discrimination, including rehabilitation schemes. As well, former officers of the battalion emerged as leaders in native affairs following the war.[10]

United States

The Indians of the United States have a proud record of service in both wars. During the First World War, of an estimated Indian population of some 330,000 about 10,000 served: 6,500 were drafted into the army, 2,000 volunteered for army service in the United States or Canada, 1,000 were in the U.S. Navy and the remainder in other services. Upwards of three hundred were killed, and over fifty were decorated.[11] As the United States did not enter the war until April 1917, some native Americans joined and served overseas with the Canadian Expeditionary Force. While no precise statistics are available, it appears that more U.S. Indians enlisted in Canada in World War I than in World War II, whereas more Canadian Indians enlisted in the United States in the Second World War than in the First. In 1917 not all Indians of the United States held American citizenship. Thus, those who were not citizens were exempted from selective service laws. In 1924, all American Indians were conferred certificates of citizenship. During the Second World War, all eligible American Indian males between ages twenty-one and forty-four were subject to the draft and larger numbers were inducted into the armed forces than in 1917-18. American Indian support, however, was not based on compulsion but rather on a willingness to serve. So great was the response of the Indians that their participation became part of American folklore.

A small minority of American Indians, however, refused to register for the draft in the Second World War. Some Seminoles claimed that they had never made peace with the United States and thus were still technically at war. Some of the Iroquois in the United States objected on the grounds that they were an independent nation. This position was argued in 1941 by Warren Green, member of the Six Nations from New York State, before a U.S. Circuit Court of Appeals. The court ruled that Iroquois Confederacy members who resided in the United States were citizens of that country and subject to American laws, including the Selective Service Act.

The American Indian effort in World War II was outstanding. Of a registered population of 287,970 some 25,000 Indians served in the American forces, almost 22,000 in the Army, with 483 losing their lives. More than 200 received awards and decorations.[12]

While the Indian population of the United States is larger than that of Canada, it is scattered in a country with a greater population. Nevertheless, in the Second World War, servicemen of Indian ancestry could rise to much higher positions in the American than in the Canadian forces. This is largely because in the United States they were more integrated in American society.

C.L. Tinker

The first American general killed in the Second World War was Major General Clarence Leonard Tinker of the U.S. Army Air Force. He was lost at Midway, June 7, 1942, when his aircraft went out of control and crashed into the sea.[13] He was posthumously awarded the Distinguished Service Medal. Of Osage ancestry, Tinker is sometimes referred to as the first American of Indian descent to become a general in World War II.

J.J. Clark

Another American with Indian ancestry, Joseph James Clark (1893-1971), one quarter Cherokee from Pryor and Chelsea, Oklahoma, became a prominent naval officer. He graduated from Annapolis Naval Academy and served briefly in World War I in the U.S. Navy. He served as an instructor at the Naval Academy in 1923-24 and later qualified as a naval aviator. Distinguished service in World War II, particulary in command of the new carrier *Yorktown* in the Pacific, helped him attain the rank of rear admiral, 31 January 1944. 'Jocko' Clark retired in December 1953 as an admiral. For many years he was a prominent business executive in New York City.[14]

E.E. Evans

A naval officer with Indian ancestry who received the Medal of Honor was Ernest E. Evans (1908-1944) of Pawnee, Oklahoma. Evans was appointed from the navy at large to the Naval Academy at Annapolis in 1927. Following graduation with a Bachelor of Science degree, he was commissioned as an ensign and served on a succession of ships. As commander of a destroyer, the U.S.S. *Johnston,* he engaged Japanese battleships that were attempting to strike a severe blow against the U.S. Navy and disrupt the landing by American troops in the Philippines. Evans was lost with 185 members of the ship's 327 men crew. Through the efforts of the *Johnston* and other ships, the Japanese force was slowed down and turned back.[15]

Ernest Childers and Jack Montgomery

Two Indian officers in the U.S. Army from Oklahoma, Lieutenant Ernest Childers, a Creek, and Lieutenant Jack Montgomery, a Cherokee, were also

Navajo Marines, using their own language as a code, transmit
messages in the dense jungle of Bouganville, December 1943. (U.S.
Marine Corps.)

awarded the Medal of Honor, their country's highest award for bravery. Ernest Childers made the Army a career. He also worked for the Department of the Interior of Washington. Following the war, Jack Montgomery was employed as an instructor in the Army and by the Veterans Administration in Oklahoma. Both men, now friends, are happily retired and live in Coweta and Gore, Oklahoma, where they are highly esteemed.

Ira Hayes

Perhaps the Indian soldier best known to the North American public is Ira H. Hayes. A Pima from the Gila River reservation in Arizona, he appears in the famous photograph showing the Marines raising the Stars and Stripes on Iwo Jima. The photo so captured the American public's imagination that Hayes became a national hero and was returned to the United States to promote the sale of war bonds. Sad to relate, following his discharge Hayes became a destitute alcoholic on the streets of Chicago and was frequently arrested for vagrancy and drunkenness. He was found dead at age 32 of alcoholism and exposure in the desert on his reserve. To many North Americans the life of Ira Hayes became an example of the fate of Indians who fought for their country. Here was one who symbolized the American spirit yet never realized the American dream.

A motion picture, *The Outsider* (1961), starring Tony Curtis as Hayes, attempted to tell Hayes' story. The American country singer, Johnny Cash, further publicized him in 1964 in a best-selling record, the *Ballad of Ira Hayes*.

The Navajo Code Talkers

While Ira Hayes became a well publicized symbol of the maltreatment of the American Indian, Navajo Indians of the U.S. Marines who conducted radio communication in their own language in the South Pacific helped to exemplify the American Indian contribution during the war more positively. The Japanese were never able to find an interpreter as the Navajo language was virtually unknown to outsiders.[16]

While the Navajos have received much deserved acclaim, the contribution of Canadian Indians in general, or even a specific group such as the Six Nations of the Grand River near Brantford, Ontario, have been unrecognized. The occasional Canadian newspaper story that appears on this subject usually concentrates on alleged injustices.[17]

Alaska Territorial Guard

Japanese actions on the Pacific prompted defence measures in Alaska. Some of the native people there were drafted into the army but most served in the local defence force, the Alaska Territorial Guard. It was formed early in the war to watch the coast, assist the armed forces in rescue missions and to help in case of enemy attack. Several thousand Indians, Eskimos* and Aleuts were among its members. A small elite unit of this force, the Alaska Scouts, also had a considerable proportion of native people.[18] The support given to the Alaska Territorial Guard by the native peoples of Alaska exemplified their overwhelming loyalty and willingness to serve.

*In Alaska, the term Eskimo is still commonly used.

Eskimos of the Alaska Territorial Guard training at Port Hope in 1943. (Fort Richardson)

CONCLUSION

About 3,500 treaty Indians probably enlisted of an Indian population of about 106,500[1] in the First World War and of these I would estimate that over 300 were killed. According to the records of Indian Affairs, during the Second World War of an estimated 126,000[2] Indians in Canada, total enlistments were 3,090 treaty Indians in the Canadian forces. Of this number over 200 were killed or died of wounds.[3] I would estimate enlistments and fatalities as being higher.

During both World Wars the enlistment of treaty Indians was encouraged by the government. They responded in numbers far greater than their treatment had merited. In the battles they fought exceptionally well and suffered heavy casualties; when peace came, they did not share to the same extent in the material benefits of the society.

Perhaps the two most traumatic events of the 20th century have been the two World Wars. Their effects were felt all over the globe. They brought significant change to this country and its people, including our native people. While the difficulties of adjusting to military life were generally more difficult for native recruits in the First World War, the social impact of the Second World War was perhaps greater.

Industrialization and urbanization, the further opening up of remote areas, better communication and the increased influence of the white man and his culture, had a significant effect. Between 1914 and 1945 numerous changes occurred to families as well as to reserves. The period was one of cultural assimilation as well as adaptation.

Some believe that Indians did not constitute good soldier material; others claim they were all excellent soldiers. Colonel J.R. Stone, DSO, MC, who commanded a battalion both in the Second World War and in Korea, offers an opinion based on experience: "The Indian and Metis soldiers served just as well as the others. There were just as many drunks and deadbeats among them and just as many disciplined soldiers."[4] Dr. (formerly Captain) George Stanley, the noted military historian, recalls:

At the Training Centre at Fredericton in 1941, I had a number of Micmacs and Maliseets. They were excellent as parade ground soldiers. I even used a platoon of Indians as a guard-of-honour for the opening of the Legislature. They put on an excellent show—good coordination and very steady. They were well motivated because they liked and respected the officers and non-commissioned officers under whom they served. I think it was a matter of winning their respect; and doing so by fairness and understanding....

The Indians were, however, always on the alert to take offence. They seemed to anticipate that the 'whites' would not like them and would treat them badly. It took time to overcome this attitude. Perhaps I was fortunate in winning their cooperation by defending one of them in a court martial. The Indian was absent three months and charged with desertion. My defence was based on two points.

(1) The Indian's cultural background was different from ours. He was not used to working with others and spending long periods drilling and training for war. His idea of fighting was to take a rifle and go off to find the enemy. His cultural pattern was not based on group discipline which he found boring. So he went absent without leave until the Army was ready to send him overseas to fight.

(2) My second line of defence (and probably the most effective) was the fact that he was picked up on his reserve still wearing a uniform. Desertion requires proof of intent to desert. The best proof of intent would be the discarding of the uniform. Since the Indian, when taken into custody, was still in uniform, it was obvious there was no intent to desert. I scolded the military police for taking three months before they thought to go to the Indian reserve. Where else would an Indian go but back to his reserve?

The court gave the Indian two weeks confinement to the guard house. Since he had spent eleven days awaiting trial he had to spend only three more days in the clink. After that, my stock with the Indians was pretty high.

One night I heard a row in one of the barrack blocks. I went with my Company Sergeant-Major. I found a group of Indians and whites just about ready for a battle. On the floor was a drunken Indian boy. The white corporal said the Indian had returned drunk and disorderly and he had ordered him to be escorted to the guard room by two privates (whites). I asked the senior Indian present what he had to say. He said the young Indian was drunk and should be taken to the guard room. What they were afraid of was that he would be beaten up by the white escort. I told the corporal to appoint an escort of one white man and one Indian to take the boy to the guard room. That solved the crisis. Indians have so often been beaten up by whites that they were suspicious of white soldiers and white officers....[5]

In the Second World War, as in the First, most Indian recruits were familiar with firearms and the outdoors. Like their ancestors, many were excellent marksmen. Indians served in a wide variety of roles in the army, navy and air force. Their record in the 1939-45 war reflects a wide range of skills and interests (not just sniping and scouting) to which fatal casualties and the circumstances of their deaths bear witness.

The contribution of our native people as scouts and snipers, however, should not be forgotten. Their record in this area, particularly in the First World War, is unsurpassed.

What surprised me most in the course of my research was the prevalence still of enduring patriotism among native veterans and their families in spite of wartime sacrifices. Although there was some bitterness and anger about past involvement in both World Wars,[6] I found that most viewed their war service with pride.

It is not surprising that some Indian veterans of both World Wars should harbour resentment. On the one hand they had been actively recruited and encouraged to volunteer for service overseas; yet many found, when they returned home, that their lot had not improved and their contribution was already forgotten.

Some maintain that Canada's Indian soldiers who were killed, particularly during the First World War, were "dying for a cause and not knowing what that cause was and not even understanding that cause."[7] Although this may be true in part for some Indians and non-Indians alike, it hardly applies to all. My research indicates that although many did not know all the facts either in 1914 or in 1939, it was sufficient for them that a state of war existed. They knew this country was at war and they wanted to serve. If necessary, they were willing to lay down their lives. They enlisted and many went overseas in spite of objections and protests from some Indian leaders and loved ones. We who enjoy the benefits of living in Canada and those countries that they helped defend and liberate are forever indebted to them. Let us hope that their sacrifice will not be forgotten.

Beny-sur-Mer Cemetery in Normandy. (Veterans Affairs)

NOTES

Part 1   The First World War

1. Honours and Awards, Veterans Affairs. This is the source of all further First World War citations.
2. Public Archives of Canada (PAC), Record Group (RG) 24, Volume (V) 1221, file HQ 593-1-7, telegram from the Adjutant General to Colonel L.W. Shannon, August 8, 1914; RG 10, Vol. 6766, file 452-13: Department of Militia and Defence to Deputy Minister, Department of Indian Affairs, October 22, 1915.
3. *Annual Report of the Department of Indian Affairs for the Year Ended March 31, 1919,* Ottawa 1920, p. 13.
4. Joseph Chaballe, *Histoire du 22e bataillon canadien-francais, 1914, 1919,* Tome 1, p. 289.
5. RG 7, G21, Vol. 549, file 104071F.
6. *Ibid.*
7. RG 24, Vol. 4383, file 2D, 34-7-109.
8. G.F.G. Stanley, "The Significance of the Six Nations Participation in the War of 1812", *Ontario History,* LV, No 4 (December 1963), pp. 215-221.
9. RG 9, III, Vol. 4931, Folder 410, War Diary, 21st Battalion, 9-3-18, p. 240.
10. RG 10, Vol. 6784, file 452-390.
11. RG 10, Vol. 6771, file 452-29.
12. *Ibid.*
13. *Ibid.*
14. RG 10, Vol. 6771, file 452-29, September 14, 1918, letter to Father John.
15. *Ibid.*
16. *Ibid,* Indian Agent to Duncan Scott, Deputy Superintendent General of Indian Affairs, January 1, 1919.
17. *Annual Report of the Department of Indian Affairs for the Year Ended March 31, 1919,* Ottawa 1920, p. 26.
18. RG 10, Vol. 4070, file 427, 063-A3. Directorate of History, National Defence Headquarters, Ottawa, C.E.F. Officers Records of Service, Vol. 6.
19. RG 9, III, Vol. 5010, War Diary, 107th Pioneer Battalion.
20. See Grant MacEwan, *Fifty Mighty Men,* Saskatoon, Modern Press, 1958, pp. 116-122.
21. RG 9, III, Vol 5010, War Diary, 107th Battalion.
22. J.C. Wise, "The American Indians in the World War", U.S. Army Military History Institute, n.d., unpublished, p. 14.
23. *Ibid.,* p. 28 (See Appendix A).
24. Tom Holm, "Fighting a White Man's War: the Extent and Legacy of American Indian Participation in World War II", *The Journal of Ethnic Studies,* (Summer 1981) p. 71.
25. RG 10, Vol. 6785, file 452-403, December 16, 1920.
26. Victor W. Wheeler, *The 50th Battalion in No Man's Land,* Calgary, Alberta Historical Resources Foundation, p. 322.
27. Interview with Duncan Pegahmagabow, 18 January 1983; John Macfie "A fighting man called Peggy was a war hero", *Parry Sound Beacon,* 11 November 1982.
28. RG 10, Vol. 6767, file 452-15, part 1.
29. RG 10, Vol. 6771, file 452-29.
30. RG 10, Vol. 6768, file 452-20, part 1, November 1917.
31. *Ibid.,* part 2.
32. *Ibid.,* RG 10, Vol. 6770, file 452-26, part 1.
33. RG 10, Vol. 6770, file 452-24.
34. RG 10, Vol. 6771, file 452-30: John Hawksley, Indian Superintendent, Dawson, Y.T., to J.D. McLean

Assistant Deputy and Secretary, Department of Indian Affairs, Ottawa, March 8, 1919.

35. Duncan Campbell Scott, "The Canadian Indians and the Great World War", *Guarding the Channel Ports,* Vol. III of Canada in the Great World War, Toronto, 1919, pp. 285-329.

36. RG 10, Vol. 6765, file 452-7, recruiting by Charles A Cooke, 1916-17.

37. *Ibid.*

38. RG 10, Vol. 6766, file 452-13, 20 October - December 1917.

39. RG 10, Vol. 6771, file 452-29, 17 December 1918.

Part II Between the Wars

1. John Hawkes, *The Story of Saskatchewan and its People* (Chicago 1924), pp. 1196-7; RG 10, Vol. 4070, file 427,063-A.

2. Donald B. Smith, *Long Lance* (Toronto 1982), p. 93 (see footnote 7); RG 10, Vol. 4070, file 427,063-A, Graham file, 1909-1914.

3. RG 10, Vol. 6766, file 452-14, Part I; RG 10, Vol. 4069, file 427,063; RG 10, Vol. 4070, file 427,063-A; *Annual Report of the Department of Indian Affairs for the Year Ended March 31, 1919* (Ottawa: King's Printer, 1920) p. 10.

4. See Regina, *Leader Post,* January 1, 1921.

5. RG 10, Vol. 4070, file 427,063-A, Graham file, 1909-1944: J.A. Newnham to Duncan Scott.

6. *Indian Veterans' Rights,* Legal Information Service, University of Saskatchewan, Native Law Centre, Report No. 3, 1979, p. 5; RG 10, Vol. 4048, file 357, 579.

7. *Sixth Report of the Soldier Settlement Board of Canada,* December 31, 1927, p. 7.

8. Robert Craig Brown and Ramsay Cook, *Canada, 1896-1921; A Nation Transformed* (Toronto 1974), p.326; William M. Drummond, "Financing of Land Settlement in Canada" (unpublished manuscript, University of Toronto Library, n.d.), p. 310.

9. *Soldier Settlement on the Land; Report of the Soldier Settlement Board of Canada,* March 31, 1921, p. 104; 10. RG 10, Vol. 7526, file 25, 116-3, Pt. 1.

10. RG 10, Vol. 4048, file 357,579, August 23, 1934.

11. RG 10, Vol. 6771, file 452-32, Pt. 1: Tucker to G.L. Drew, Vocational Officer for Ontario, Toronto, October 8, 1919.

12. RG 10, Vol. 6773, file 452-61: memorandum signed by H.F. Bury, Windsor Junction, Nova Scotia, March 7, 1919, to the Chief Accountant, Ottawa.

13. RG 10, Vol. 6771, file 452-30, September 3, 1919.

14. RG 10, Vol. 6787, file 452-453.

15. RG 10, Vol. 6772, file 452-40.

16. RG 10, Vol. 6762, file 452-1, Pt. 5: Murray MacLaren, MD, Minister of Pensions and National Health, Ottawa, to T.G. Murphy, Superintendent General of Indian Affairs, 5 April 1932.

17. Walter S. Woods, *Rehabilitation (A Combined Operation)* Ottawa, 1953, p. 29.

18. RG 10, Vol. 6772, file 452-40: Harold McGill, Deputy Superintendent General, circular to all Indian Agents, 12 May 1936.

19. RG 10, Vol. 6772, file 452-40, April 20, 1936.

20. *Ibid.* May 27, 1936.

21. RG 10, Vol. 6771, file 452-37: Morgan to Secretary, Department of Indian Affairs, Ottawa, January 17, 1933.

22. RG 10, Vol. 6771, file 452-37, 7 February 1936: J.C.G. Herwig, Service Bureau, the Canadian Legion..., Dominion headquarters, Ottawa, to R.E. Wodehouse, Deputy Minister of Pensions and National Health, Ottawa.

23. *Ibid.*

24. RG 10, Vol. 6771, file 452-37: Herwig to Wodehouse, Ottawa, 8 February, 1936.

25. *Ibid.,* March and April 1936.

Part III The Second World War

1. RG 10, Vol. 6764, file 452-6, Pt 2; *Regina Leader Post,* 14 October 1939, 10 October 1940, 8 July 1941; *Toronto Globe and Mail,* 31 January 1942.

2. W. Boss, *The Stormont, Dundas and Glengarry Highlanders, 1783-1951* (Ottawa 1952), p. 165.

3.   Second World War citations can be found at the Directorate of History, National Defence Headquarters, Ottawa.

4.   G.R. Stevens, *A City Goes to War* (Brampton, Ontario, 1964), p. 274.

5.   Letter, Colonel J.R. Stone to Fred Gaffen, 8 March 1982.

6.   Thomas H. Raddall, *West Novas, A History of the West Nova Scotia Regiment* (Liverpool, N.S. 1947), pp. 180-1.

7.   Farley Mowat, *The Regiment* (Toronto 1973), p. 242.

8.   Letter from G.F.G. Stanley to Fred Gaffen, 13 October 1982.

9.   Doris A. Paul, *The Navajo Code Talkers* (Philadelphia 1973), p. 9.

10. Letter from D. Charles MacDougall to Fred Gaffen, 14 January 1983.

11. *The Argyll and Sutherland Highlanders of Canada (Princess Louise's), 1928-1953.* Compiled by officers of the Regiment. Edited by H.M. Jackson (Montreal 1953), p. 206.

12. "Jottings from a Record of Service in the North-West Campaign, July 9th, 1944-May 8th, 1945" by Gnr. J.P. Brady. Brady Papers, Glenbow Archives.

13. See Murray Dobbin, *The One-And-A-Half Men: the Story of Jim Brady and Malcolm Norris, Metis Patriots of the Twentieth Century,* Vancouver 1981.

14. Interview with Albert R. Corston, RCAF Officers' Mess, Ottawa, 18 September 1981.

15. *Badges of the Canadian forces/Les insignes des forces canadiennes* (Ottawa: DND, 1976).

16. RG 10, Vol. 6770, file 452-26.

17. RG 10, Vol. 6768, file 452-20, Pt. 4, June 22, 1943.

18. RG 10, Vol. 6769, file 452-20-10.

19. RG 10, Vol. 6769, file 452-20, Pt. 6: Arnold Heeney, Clerk of the Privy Council to T.A. Crerar, Minister of Mines and Resources, 26 December 1944.

20. Indian Affairs (RG 10, Volume 6769, file 452-20, Pt.6).

21. See *Calgary Herald, Ottawa Citizen,* June 23, 1942.

22. RG 10, Vol. 6773, file 452-48.

23. *The Indian Missionary Record,* October 15, 1942, p. 1.

24. F.J. Niven, "Canada's Indians are helping with many tons of Buffalo Bones", *Saturday Night,* LIX (June 10, 1944), p. 37.

25. RG 10, Vol. 6761, file 452-20, Part 4, August 12, 1943.

26. RG 10, Vol. 6772, file 452-42 *(Alberta Inspectorate Report for Fiscal Year Ending March 31, 1943,* by C.P. Schmidt, Inspector of Indian Agencies, Alberta Inspectorate).

27. RG 10, Vol. 6772, file 452-42.

28. *The Canadian Indian; The Prairie Provinces* (Indian Affairs and Northern Development, 1980), p. 17.

29. A.R. Paudash, "I Married an Indian", *Maclean's Magazine,* LIV (December 1, 1951), p. 28.

30. *Ibid.* p. 28.

31. Conversation with Fred Gaffen, 29 January 1983.

32. RG 10, Vol. 7533, file 26,107-3, Pt. 1: J.C. Caldwell, Chief Reserve Division to Dr. H.W. McGill, Department of Mines and Resources, Indian Affairs Branch, April 6, 1939.

33. RG 10, Vol. 7534, file 26,118-5: T.A. Crerar to Secretary-Treasurer, St. Paul Branch (No 100) Canadian Legion, St. Paul, Alberta, January 25, 1944.

34. RG 10, Vol. 6771, file 452-32, Pt. 2, 7 September 1945; Walter S. Woods, *Rehabilitation (A Combined Operation),* (Ottawa 1953), pp. 142-146.

35. Kate Fawkes, "The Veterans Land Act: Its Application with regard to Indian Veterans". Research paper, prepared for the Department of Indian Affairs, 1980.

36. *Indians in the War [1941-1945]* (Chicago 1945), p. 46.

37. Department of Indian Affairs, Veterans' Land Act, General Headquarters, Vol. 4, file 39/6.

38. J.R. Ponting and Roger Gibbins, *Out of Irrelevance* (Calgary 1980), p. 235.

39. See Murray Dobbin, *The One-And-A-Half Men: the Story of Jim Brady and Malcolm Norris, Metis Patriots of the Twentieth Century* (Vancouver 1981).

40. Bruce Sealey, ed., *Famous Manitoba Metis* (Winnipeg 1974), pp. 75-6.

41. *A Pictorial History of the Metis and Non-Status Indians in Saskatchewan* (Saskatchewan Human Rights Commission, 1976), pp. 32, 36, 40.

42. See Terrance Lusty, *Metis, Social-Political Movement* (Calgary, Metis Historical Society, 1973), p. 16.

Part IV A Comparison with Native Peoples in Australia, New Zealand and the United States

1. C.E.W. Bean, *Anzac to Amiens: A Shorter History of the Australian Fighting Services in the First World War* (Canberra 1961), p. 532.
2. C.D. Clark, "Aborigines in the First AIF", *Australian Army Journal,* No. 286, (March 1973), p. 22.
3. See Gavin Long, *The Final Campaigns.* Series I, Vol. VII of Australia in the War of 1939-1945 (Canberra 1963); Norman Bartlett, ed., *With the Australians in Korea* (Canberra 1954) and Harry Gordon, *The Embarrassing Australian; the Story of an Aboriginal Warrior* (London 1963).
4. R.A. Hall, "Aborigines and the Army; the Second World War Experience" [Australian] *Defence Force Journal,* (September - October, 1980), p. 31.
5. R.A. Hall, p. 39. Australian Archives, supplementary notes to "Preliminary Outline of Proposals for Education and Welfare of Natives of NT Force".
6. James Cowan, *The Maoris in the Great War* (Wellington 1926), p. 8.
7. J.F. Cody, *28th (Maori Battalion)* (Wellington 1956), p. 501.
8. Letter, Department of Internal Affairs, Historical Branch, Wellington, 6 July 1982; Letter, Ministry of Defence, Wellington, 1 September 1982.
9. Kenneth R. Hancock, *New Zealand at War* (Wellington 1946), pp. 274-277.
10. Michael King, *New Zealanders at War* (Auckland 1981), p. 3.
11. "The American Indian in the World War", Bulletin 15, 1927, U.S. Department of the Interior, Office of Indian Affairs; Letter, U.S. Army Military History Institute, Carlisle Barracks, Pa., U.S.A., 1 September 1982.
12. *Indians in the War* [1941-1945]. Chicago: United States Department of the Interior, Office of Indian Affairs, 1945.
13. F.O. DuPre, *U.S. Air Force Biographical Dictionary* (New York 1965), pp. 235-6.
14. See J.J. Clark with C.G. Reynolds, *Carrier Admiral* (New York 1967).
15. Biographies Branch, U.S. Naval Historical Center, Navy Yard, Washington, D.C.
16. See Doris A. Paul, *The Navajo Code Talkers* (Philadelphia 1973).
17. *Edmonton Journal,* 11 November 1982, A2, E10.
18. Stan Cohen, *The Forgotten War: a Pictorial History of World War II in Alaska and Northwestern Canada* (Missoula, Montana 1981), pp. 95-97.

NOTES

Conclusion

1. Census of Indians, Department of Indian Affairs, *Canada, Sessional Paper No. 27; Sixth Census of Canada, 1921,* Vol. I (Ottawa 1924), Population 1921, 1911, and 1901 in Table 23.
2. *Census of Indians in Canada, 1944,* Ottawa: Department of Mines and Resources, Indian Affairs Branch, King's Printer, 1945.
3. Department of Indian Affairs, File 1/39-6; Executive Assistant to E.L. Stone, 1 November 1947.
4. Letter to author, 8 March 1982.
5. Letter to author, 13 October 1982.
6. See videocassette held by Theytus of the Third British Columbia Indian Veterans' Reunion, Chulus Hall, Merritt, 4-5 June 1983.

   "...We were told how great it was that we volunteered to serve and fight overseas, yet once back home, we still faced discrimination."

   Ottawa Citizen, 27 October 1983, p. 31. John Tootoosis, representing the Federation of Saskatchewan Indians, told a conference on aging: "I'm sure you can afford good housing for Indian old people from what you have developed out of our land. We lost a lot of Indian boys for you in two World Wars, and the ones who came back were just given a piece of land that was already theirs before they left. I hope you appreciate what they did."
7. See *Indian News,* Vol. 22, No. 8, November 1981, Wallace LaBillois, resident elder, National Indian Brotherhood and a director of the National Indian Veterans Association to A/Editor, Rob Belfry.

*Report on Indians in the American forces
by Lieutenant J. R. Eddy, U.S. Army*

DIGEST OF OPINIONS

Generally:

1. Does he stand the nervous strain?
HE DOES.

2. Does he prove a natural leader in ranks?
HE DOES NOT.

3. Does he associate readily with white men?
HE DOES.

4. Is he regarded by the whites as an unusually "good" man?
HE IS REGARDED AS A VERY GOOD SOLDIER.

5. Has he demonstrated fitness for any special arm?
AUTOMATIC WEAPONS.

Scouting:

6. What capacity has he shown under the following heads?

a) Courage; endurance; good humour.
VERY GOOD IN ALL.

b) Keenness of senses; dexterity.
GOOD IN BOTH.

c) Judgement and initiative.
FAIR IN BOTH.

d) Ability to utilize mechanical methods, maps, buzzers, etc.
POOR IN ALL.

e) As night worker, runner, observer and verbal reporter.
GOOD IN ALL EXCEPTING THE LAST; A POOR VERBAL REPORTER.

Indian Self-Confidence.

When questioned as to their ability to maintain direction and to find their way about night or day in open country or in woods the almost invariable answer of many Indians interrogated was to the effect that they always felt quite sure of their direction.

The Indian ascribes his generally constant individual orientation to quick mental adjustment of terrain relationship resulting from habitual observation of wind, sun, moon, stars, landmarks, memory of country traversed, and to knowledge of woodcraft.

Blindfolded ... in an intelligence section group under training in an open woods, Indians were the only scouts in the exercise able to reach previously indicated objectives 100 feet ahead. These were attained by carefully crawling, feeling out the ground and growth along the course, and by memory picture of the intervening terrain. These tests were repeatedly made in intelligence training in the 36th Division.

Utilization of the Indian as a Scout.

Analysis of data covering reports on representatives of above forty tribes indicates that the Indian, apart from being a good soldier, possesses characteristics making him particularly valuable for scouting personnel.

He proves to be a good athlete, shows remarkable sense of direction, goes about his duties uncomplainingly, does not get lost, is a good runner, has unlimited patience and reserve, is a good shot, crawls habitually on night patrols, has non-light reflective countenance at night, is silent at work, stoical under fire, and grasps the significance and makes free use of signals.

Battalion Scout Platoon.

In the battalion scout platoon the Indian soldier of average education may be trained to acquire facility in handling maps, mechanical methods, buzzers, etc. Here, too, he will receive the instruction given to all scouts, snipers and observers in the scout platoon.

The fact that the Indian has not shown facility with the above specified equipment of the battalion scout section is due largely to lack of sufficient training with these materials. The educated Indian soldier, given an opportunity to acquire knowledge of these devices, will prove able to handle them efficiently.

With repect to verbal message transmission, it may be said that in a Division where special exercises and training was given to develop ability to accurately transmit verbal messages, educated Indian soldiers showed up remarkably well in verbal message transmission tests.

Maneuvers.

If detailed to act as scouts and guides in problems involving attack, the example set by the Indians in making aggressive use of cover and low crouching advance will stimulate men of ranks to assume similar methods of approach.

Special Tactical Value.

In war of movement Indians should be used as guides and scouts to orient the advance of platoons and platoon sections into attack. They should be detailed to this service from the battalion scout platoon.

The compass, upon which our officers now depend for direction to advance through woods and over open country, necessitates frequent pauses for orientation, and during these pauses the officers are positive marks for enemy snipers. Indian scouts, moving from cover to cover guiding advancing groups and keeping direction without need of frequent reference to the compass will tend to hold direction for advancing units and avoid to a considerable extent the easy identification of officers and other advancing group leaders.

In war of position they should be used as guides for night patrols and as observers and snipers, and to guide troops into and out of trench positions at night.

Conclusion.

The Indian is exceptionally qualified by natural characteristics and disposition as a scout for service in modern warfare.

Recommendations.

That recognition of the scouting qualifications of the Indian be officially indicated with a view to having his services more generally made use of in the battalion scout platoons. Deserved recognition would stimulate the Indians now in the service and Indian cadets undergoing military training in the U.S. Government schools to show added interest in the Service and tend to provide excellent scouting personnel for the army."

Roll of Honour
(*Killed in Action or Died of Wounds or Accident or Disease Overseas from War Service)

First World War, 1914-1918

Private	*AARON	William	116th Battalion, August 13, 1918, Ohsweken, Ontario.
Private	*AHKWENZIE	Leslie	43rd Battalion, August 8, 1918, Saugeen Band, Chippawa Hill, Ontario.
Private	*ALEXANDER	Charles	26th Battalion, April 9, 1917, Eel Ground Band, Newcastle, New Brunswick.
Private	ALTIMAN	Gilbert	149th Battalion, January 21, 1917, Walpole Island Band, Wallaceburg, Ontario.
Private	*ANDERSON	Robert	52nd Battalion, December 30, 1917, Hiawatha, Ontario.
Private	ANDREW	Tommy (Thomas)	Canadian Forestry Corps, October 26, 1918, Little Shuswap Band, Squilax, British Columbia.
Private	*ANTOINE	David	102nd Battalion, May 18, 1917, Nipissing Band, Sturgeon Falls (Mattawa), Ontario.
Private	ARMSTRONG	Frank	149th Battalion, May 3, 1920, Walpole Island Band, Wallaceburg, Ontario.
Private	*ASHAM	Kenneth McClure	78th Battalion, March 28, 1917, Peguis Band, Hodgson, Manitoba.
Private	*ATHANASE	Joseph Arthur Thomas	22nd Battalion, May 13, 1917, Malecite, Cacouna and Riviere-du-Loup, Quebec.
Private	*BACK	Richard	42nd Battalion, April 27, 1917, St. Regis, Cornwall, Ontario.
Private	*BARDY	Frank	27th Battalion, April 10, 1917, Shannonville, Bay of Quinte, Ontario.
Private	*BARNABY (BERNABY)	Joseph	8th Battalion, September 29, 1918, Restigouche, Quebec.
Private	*BARNHART	Cornelius	2nd Battalion, December 13, 1918, Bay of Quinte, Ontario.
Private	*BARNHART	Harry	87th Battalion, November 18, 1916, Bay of Quinte, Ontario.

Private	*BEAUCHENE	Louis	50th Battalion, October 26th,1918, Medicine Hat, Alberta.
Private	*BEAUVAIS	Joseph	1st Battalion, October 1, 1918, Oka Band, Oka, Quebec.
*Private	*BEGGS	Adolphus Henry	52nd Battalion, September 4, 1917, Kenora, Ontario.
Private	*BEAVER	Austin Henry	18th Battalion, February 22, 1917, Alderville Band, Roseneath, Ontario.
Private	*BELANGER	Augustin, MM	52nd Battalion, May 25, 1917, Fort William, Ontario.
Private	*BERNARD	James	58th Battalion, September 19, 1918, Bayfield Road, Nova Scotia.
Private	*BERNARD	Stephen	87th Battalion, August 11, 1917, Burnt Church Band, Lagaceville, New Brunswick.
Private	BEYNON	Richard Arthur	103rd Battalion, December 22, 1918, Port Simpson Band, Victoria, British Columbia.
Private	*BIGMAN	Alexander	46th Battalion, February 6, 1917, Battleford, Saskatchewan.
Private	*BIGNELL	Paul	Canadian Forestry Corps, February 1, 1919, The Pas, Manitoba.
Private	*BLACKFACE	George	8th Battalion, September 29, 1918, Bird Tail Sioux, Beulah, Manitoba.
Private	*BLAKER	Victor W.	Princess Patricia's Canadian Light Infantry, October 30, 1917, Alderville Band, Roseneath, Ontario.
Private	*BLAKER	William	5th Battalion, April 5, 1917, Alderville Band, Roseneath, Ontario.
Private	BLOOMFIELD	Frederick	243rd Battalion, February 6, 1917, Muskoday Band near Birch Hills, Saskatchewan.
Sapper	*BOLDUC	Joseph T.	1st Bridging Company, Canadian Railway Troops, October 25, 1918, Chapleau, Ontario (buried in Egypt).
Private	*BONE	Antoine	107th Pioneer Battalion, August 15, 1917, Camperville, Manitoba.
Private	BONES	John	18th Reserve Battalion, Manitou Rapids Band, February 22, 1919, Barwick, Ontario.
Private	BOUCHE[R]	Lawrence	Canadian Forestry Corps, December 17, 1917, Fort William Band, near Thunder Bay, Ontario.
Lieutenant	*BRANT	Cameron D.	4th Battalion, April 24, 1915, New Credit Band, Hagersville and also a resident of Hamilton, Ontario.
Private	*BRANT	Charles Arthur	15th Battalion, August 15, 1917, Bay of Quinte, Ontario.

Private	*BRANT	Ernest Russell	28th Battalion, August 16, 1918, Bay of Quinte, Ontario.
Private	*BRANT	Richard	2nd Battalion, May 3, 1917, Shannonville, Bay of Quinte, Ontario.
Private	*BREWER	William	47th Battalion, January 9, 1918, Okanagan Band, Vernon, British Columbia.
Private	*CADA	Michael	54th Battalion, September 30, 1918, Manitoulin Island, Ontario.
Private	*CAMERON	James	5th Canadian Mounted Rifles, April 9, 1917, Restigouche Band, Restigouche, Quebec.
Private	*CAMERON	Roderick	27th Battalion, September 15, 1916, Lac Seul, Ontario.
Private	CANADA	Charles	233rd Battalion, December 27, 1916, Cumberland House, Saskatchewan.
Private	CAPLEN	Charles	145th Battalion, July 8, 1917, Lennox Island, Prince Edward Island.
Private	*CHAKAS-UAM	(Nona) Laurent	Canadian Forestry Corps, July 7, 1918, Fort Albany Band, James Bay, Ontario.
Private	*CHAPPISE	Peter	3rd Battalion, June 13, 1916, Chapleau, Ontario.
Private	CHARTERS	Thomas	54th Battalion, October 12, 1916, Kamloops, British Columbia.
Sapper	*CHARTRAND	Alfred	Canadian Engineers, May 31, 1918, Waterhen Band, Skownan, Manitoba.
Private	CHASKE	John	Depot Battalion, Manitoba Regiment, November 25, 1918, Sioux Village, Manitoba.
Sapper	*CHEECHOO	Alfred	Canadian Railway Troops, February 12, 1919, Moose Factory, James Bay, Ontario.
Private	*CHIEF	Alexander	52nd Battalion, December 8, 1918, (died of wounds) Savant Lake near Sioux Lookout, Ontario.
Private	CHUBB	Joseph C.	235th Battalion, October 20, 1918, Hagersville, Ontario.
Private	CLAUSE	Ambrose	155th Battalion, July 10, 1920, Bay of Quinte, Shannonville, Ontario.
Private	*CLAUSE	Isaac	1st Battalion, November 6, 1917, Brantford, Ontario.
Private	COCHRANE	Percy	28th Battalion, April 18,1918, The Pas, Manitoba.
Private	*COMEGO	Sampson	21st Battalion, November 10, 1915, Alderville Band, Roseneath, Ontario.

Private	*COMING-SINGER	George	50th Battalion, January 14, 1919, Blood Reserve, Alberta.
Private	*COMMAND-ANT	Samuel	1st Battalion, August 30, 1918, Gibson Band, Sahanatien, Ontario.
Private	*CONDO	Barney	58th Battalion, August 30, 1917, Micmacs of Maria Band, Maria and Grand-Cascapedia, Quebec.
Private	*CONSTANT	Lazarus	2nd Battalion, September 30, 1918. The Pas, Manitoba.
Private	*COOK	Albert	Lord Strathcona's Horse, May 24, 1915, St. Peters and Bloodvein, Manitoba.
Private	*COOK	Edwin Victor, DCM	7th Battalion, August 28, 1918, Nimpkish Band, Alert Bay, British Columbia.
Private	*COOK	Reynold	107th Pioneer Battalion, August 15, 1917, Fisher River Band, The Halfway, Manitoba.
Private	*COPE	James	25th Battalion, April 17, 1918, Shubenacadie Band, Truro and Windsor Junction, Nova Scotia.
Private	*CORNELIUS	Walter	5th Canadian Mounted Rifles, October 30, 1917, Oneidas of the Thames, Southwold and Fairmount, Ontario.
Private	*CROMARTY	Murdo	107th Pioneer Battalion, April 20, 1917, Norway House, Manitoba.
Private	*CROW	Joseph	46th Battalion, March 22, 1917, Cote Band, Kamsack, Saskatchewan.
Private	*CROW	William	87th Battalion, October 21, 1916, Essex, Ontario.
Private	*CURLEY	Lloyd Clifford	107th Pioneer Battalion, August 15, 1917, Ohsweken, Ontario.
Private	*DANIELS	Walter Norrsey	1st Canadian Mounted Rifles, December 3, 1916, St. Peters Band, Selkirk, Manitoba.
Private	DECAIRE	Samuel	19th Battalion, August 1, 1918, Mattawa, Ontario.
Private	*DECOTEAU	Alexander	49th Battalion, October 30, 1917, Red Pheasant Band near Battleford, Saskatchewan.
Private	DEEGAN	James	152nd Battalion, May 25, 1916, Standing Buffalo Band, Fort Qu'Appelle, Saskatchewan.
Private	*DeLARONDE	Dennis	52nd Battalion, June 1, 1916, Nipigon, Ontario.
Private	*DEMERY	Baptiste	52nd Battalion, August 10, 1918, Sandy Bay Band, Marius, Manitoba.
Private	*DENNY	John	87th Battalion, August 15, 1917, Oka, Quebec.
Private	*DEPEAU	William	2nd Battalion, September 9, 1916,

			Caughnawaga Band, Quebec.
Corporal	*DESJARLAIS	Gilbert	2nd Battalion, Canadian Engineers, October 25, 1918, Brokenhead Band, Scanterbury, Manitoba.
Private	*DESJARLAIS	Herbert	8th Battalion, August 15, 1917, Brokenhead Band, Scanterbury, Manitoba.
Private	DICK	Paul	Depot Battalion, Manitoba Regiment, May 1, 1918, Squaw Bay, Fort William, Ontario.
Private	*DICKSON	Elijah	8th Battalion, November 10, 1917, File Hills, Saskatchewan.
Private	DIX	Edward	Canadian Forestry Corps, April 26, 1920, Masset Band, Masset, British Columbia.
Corporal	*DODGE	Alexander	15th Cavalry (U.S.), May 19, 1918, Walpole Island, Wallaceburg, Ontario.
Private	*DOUGLAS	Mitchell	26th Battalion, October 14, 1916, Caughnawaga Band, Caughnawaga, Quebec.
Private	*DOXTATOR	Frederick	Canadian Engineers, November 15, 1918, Sarnia Band, Sarnia, Ontario.
Private	*DREAVER	Frank N.	5th Battalion, April 5, 1917, Mistawasis Band, Leask, Saskatchewan.
Private	*ELLIOTT	Daniel	18th Battalion, May 31, 1918, Cape Croker, Ontario.
Private	*ELLIOTT	Joseph Frank	18th Battalion, August 28, 1918, Cape Croker, Ontario
Private	*ELM	Isaac K.	4th Battalion, September 27, 1918, Oneidas of the Thames, Southwold, Ontario.
Sapper	*FISH	Reuben	Canadian Railway Troops, February 12, 1919, Six Nations, Newport, Ontario.
Private	FLAMEND	John	232nd Battalion, April 18, 1921, Muskeg Lake Band, Marcelin, Saskatchewan.
Private	*FLETT	Alexander Samuel	27th Battalion, August 22, 1917, Keeseekoowenin Band, Elphinstone, Manitoba.
Private	FLETT	George	250th Battalion, February 28, 1919, St. Peters Band, Selkirk, Manitoba.
Private	*FLETT	Solomon George	29th Battalion, July 16, 1916, Keeseekoowenin Band, Elphinstone, Manitoba.
Private	*FOXHEAD	Mike	50th Battalion, October 23, 1917, Blackfoot Band, Gleichen, Alberta.
Private	*FRANKLIN	William H.	4th Battalion, October 8, 1916, Alderville Band, Roseneath, Ontario.
Private	FRASER	John Kenneth	4th Battalion, September 27, 1920, Brantford, St. Catharines, Ontario.

97

Private	*FURLOTTE	James	42nd Battalion, April 9, 1917, Campbelltown, New Brunswick.
Lance Corporal	*GARLOW	Marshall James	1st Railway Battalion, Canadian Engineers, December 20, 1918, Hagersville, Ontario.
Private	*GASPE	James	20th Battalion, June 25, 1916, Oka, Quebec.
Private	*GEORGE	Baptist	4th Battalion, February 11, 1919, Caradoc, Ontario.
Private	*GEORGE	Wellington	75th Battalion, August 17, 1917, Oneidas of the Thames, Southwold, Ontario.
Private	*GERARD	John	46th Battalion, February 14, 1917, Muskeg Lake Band, Green Lake Saskatchewan.
Private	GLADUE	Joseph	Depot Battalion, Alberta Regiment, November 3, 1918, Beaver Lake Band, Lac La Biche, Alberta.
Private	GLODE	James	Composite Battalion, August 4, 1918, Bear River Band, Lequille, Nova Scotia.
Private	GLODE	Joseph Martin	112th Battalion, May 11, 1916, Bear River Band, Graywood, Nova Scotia.
Private	GODCHERE	Thomas, MM	102nd Battalion, April 9, 1917, Long Lac Band, Longlac, Ontario.
Private	*GOOSEY	David	107th Pioneer Battalion, April 20, 1917, Six Nations, Brantford, Ontario.
Private	*GREEN	David	1st Battalion, April 10, 1917, Deseronto, Bay of Quinte, Ontario.
Private	*GREY	Malcolm	5th Battalion, September 26, 1916, Carry the Kettle Band, Sintaluta, Saskatchewan.
Lance Corporal	*GROAT	Edward Burty	1st Battalion, October 1, 1918, Ohsweken, Ontario.
Sapper	GUSTIN	Joseph	6th Canadian Railway Troops, May 13, 1919, Moose Factory, Ontario.
Private	*GUY	James (Jimmy)	54th Battalion, March 1, 1917, Alexandria, British Columbia.
Private	*HAGAR	William	19th Battalion, May 9, 1917, Alderville Band, Roseneath, Ontario.
Private	*HAMMOND	Thomas Edward	26th Battalion, September 17, 1916, Scarsdale, Nova Scotia.
Private	*HARRIS	John	47th Battalion, August 15, 1918, Okanagan Band, Ewing, British Columbia.
Private	HIGHWAY	James	Canadian Forestry Corps, March 12, 1919, The Pas, Manitoba.
Sapper	*HILL	Hiram	1st Battalion, Canadian Engineers, July 28, 1918, Ohsweken and Hartford, Ontario.

Corporal	*HILL	Joseph Bernard, MM	5th Brigade, Canadian Field Artillery, September 30, 1918, Bay of Quinte, Ontario.
Private	*HILL	Roy	125th Battalion, December 16, 1916, Ohsweken, Ontario.
Private	*HOMER	Harrison	107th Pioneer Battalion, July 28, 1917, Ohsweken, Ontario.
Private	*HONYUST	Arthur	87th Battalion, April 14, 1917, Oneidas of the Thames, Southwold, Ontario.
Private	*HOWARD	Robert John	78th Battalion, September 25, 1918, Fort William Band, Thunder Bay, Ontario.
Sapper	ICE	Samuel	Canadian Railway Troops, August 16, 1919, Moose Factory, Ontario.
Private	ISAAC	Frank	20th Battalion, March 7, 1915, Ohsweken, Ontario.
Private	*ISAAC	Jacob	1st Battalion, August 30, 1918, Ohsweken, Ontario.
Private	ISAACS	Maurice Joseph	Canadian Forestry Corps, November 7, 1921, Columbia Lake Band, Windermere, British Columbia.
Private	*JACKSON	Philip	5th Battalion, February 1, 1917, Peepeekisis Band, Tompkins, Saskatchewan.
Private	*JAKAZOM	Peter	Canadian Forestry Corps, February 23, 1919, Attawapiskat Band, Attawapiskat, Ontario.
Private	*JAKOMOLIN	John	Canadian Forestry Corps, September 20, 1917, Fort Albany, James Bay, Ontario.
Private	*JAMES	Joseph	47th Battalion, August 22, 1917, Skookumchuck Indian Band, Mission City, British Columbia.
Private	JAMIESON	Arthur	107th Pioneer Battalion, June 2, 1917, Brantford, Ontario.
Private	*JOE	John	87th Battalion, November 16, 1917, Big Cove Reserve, Rexton, New Brunswick.
Private	*JOHN	Louis	58th Battalion, October 8, 1916, Eel Ground Reserve, Newcastle, New Brunswick and Restigouche, Quebec.
Private	*JOHN	Paul	19th Battalion, November 12, 1917, Brantford, Ontario.
Private	JOHNS	Alexander	4th Battalion, Canadian Machine Gun Corps, December 31, 1920, St. Regis, Cornwall, Ontario.
Private	JOHNSON	George	49th Battalion, April 21, 1920, Munceys of the Thames, Muncey, Ontario.
Private	*JOHNSON	John	25th Battalion, September 12, 1916, Truro, Nova Scotia.
Private	*JOHNSON	William	87th Battalion, January 2, 1918, Curve

Lake Band, Ontario.

Bombardier	JOHNSON	William Wilbur	2nd Brigade, Canadian Field Artillery, January 29, 1918, Brantford, Ontario.
Private	JOHNSTON	Archie Duncan	18th Battalion October 8, 1918, Cape Croker and Kenora, Ontario.
Private	*JOHNSTON	James W.	1st Battalion, August 30, 1918, Ohsweken and Caledonia, Ontario.
Private	*JONDREAU	Jeremiah	52nd Battalion, April 3, 1917, Hilton Band, St. Joseph Island, Ontario.
Private	JOSHUA	Daniel	187th Battalion, May 6, 1917, Samson Band, Hobbema, Alberta.
Private	KABASHK-UNG	Lazarus	47th Battalion, August 17, 1919, Saugeen Band, Chippawa Hill, Ontario.
Private	*KASTO	Thomas	27th Battalion, August 21, 1917, Oak Lake Band, Pipestone, Manitoba.
Private	*KEEASK	James	Canadian Forestry Corps, February 18, 1919, Attawapiskat Band, James Bay, Ontario.
Private	*KEESHIG	Bernard Reuben	18th Battalion, August 27, 1918, Cape Croker, Ontario.
Private	*KENNEDY	Frederick	14th Battalion, September 27, 1918, Beauval, Saskatchewan.
Private	*KEWENZIE	Isaac	46th Battalion, September 2, 1918, Saugeen Band, Chippawa Hill, Ontario.
Private	*KICK	Albert	4th Battalion, October 1, 1918, Oneidas of the Thames, Southwold, Ontario.
Private	*KIPPLING	Robert Edward	78th Battalion, April 9, 1917, St. Peters Band, Selkirk, Manitoba.
Private	*KIYOSHK	Joseph	47th Battalion, October 7, 1918, Walpole Island, Ontario.
Private	KNOCK-WOOD	Peter	25th Battalion, April 9, 1917, Lennox Island, Prince Edward Island.
Private	KOOTENAY	Albert	10th Battalion, February 11, 1919, Lac Ste. Anne, Alberta.
Private	*KUSKITCHU	John	52nd Battalion, August 28, 1918, Flying Post Band, Biscotasing, Ontario.
Private	*LAFORCE	Angus	1st Battalion, April 22, 1915, Caughnawaga Band, Caughnawaga, Quebec.
Private	LAFORME	John Alexander	114th Battalion, February 25, 1916, Hagersville, Ontario.
Private	*LAMABE	Mat	50th Battalion, November 19, 1916, Golden Lake, Ontario.
Private	*LAND	Moses	44th Battalion, November 3, 1917, Grassy Narrows, Ontario.

Private	LARIVIERE	John	98th Battalion, October 29, 1915, North Bay, Ontario.
Private	*LARIVIERE	Philippe	1st Canadian Mounted Rifles, August 11, 1918, Camperville, Manitoba.
Private	LAROCQUE	Henry	187th Battalion, January 15, 1917, Samson Band, Hobbema, Alberta.
Private	LATHLIN	Richard	2nd Battalion, October 12, 1920, The Pas, Manitoba.
Private	*LAVALLEY	Frank	1st Motor Machine Gun Brigade, September 2, 1918, Kenora, Ontario.
Private	*LAVALLEY	Peter	3rd Battalion, April 10, 1917, Golden Lake Band, resident of Whitney, Ontario.
Private	*LEIGHTON	James Newell	29th Battalion, August 27, 1917, Metlakatala Band, Prince Rupert, British Columbia.
Private	*LICKERS	Percy	107th Pioneer Battalion, August 7, 1917, Ohsweken, Ontario.
Private	*LICKERS	Thomas	2nd Battalion, April 26, 1916, Ohsweken, Ontario.
Private	*LICKERS	William	58th Battalion, October 8, 1916, Ohsweken, Ontario.
Private	*LOGAN	Arnold	1st Battalion, April 26, 1916, Chippewas of the Thames Band, Muncey, Ontario.
Private	*LOGAN	Stephen	4th Battalion, April 17, 1917, Munceys of the Thames Band, Muncey, Ontario.
Private	*LOTTRIDGE	Welby Howard	1st Battalion, August 3, 1917, Ohsweken, Ontario.
Sapper	*LUKE	William	Canadian Railway Troops, October 29, 1917, James Bay, Ontario.
Private	*LUTE	Richard	60th Battalion, September 18, 1916, St. Regis, Cornwall, Ontario.
Private	*LYONS	Thomas George	44th Battalion, August 14, 1918, Manitou Rapids, Emo, Ontario.
Private	*MAHONE	Luke Charles	47th Battalion, October 31, 1916, Nitinat and Sardis, British Columbia.
Private	*MAKOKIS	Eneas	50th Battalion, September 2, 1918, Saddle Lake, Alberta.
Private	*MALONEY	Peter	42nd Battalion, April 9, 1917, Shubenacadie Band, Hants County, Nova Scotia.
Private	*MANITO-BENIS (served as DOMINICE)	Antoine	52nd Battalion, August 17, 1918, Poplar Lodge, Lake Nipigon, Ontario.
Private	*MARACLE (served as HILL)	George Mark	1st Battalion, April 12, 1917 Bay of Quinte, Pointe Anne, Ontario.

Private	*MARACLE	Isaac	PPCLI, October 30, 1917, Shannonville, Bay of Quinte, Ontario.
Private	*MARACLE	John H.	44th Battalion, January 12, 1917, Marysville, Bay of Quinte, Ontario.
Private	*MARACLE	Peter William	52nd Battalion, October 3, 1918, Bay of Quinte, Ontario.
Private	*MARACLE	Philip	44th Battalion, May 10, 1917, Bay of Quinte, Ontario.
Private	*MARACLE	Wheeler	50th Battalion, February 3, 1917, Bay of Quinte, Ontario.
Private	*MARTIN	Lawrence	52nd Battalion, October 5, 1916, Nipigon, Ontario.
Private	*MARTIN	Walter J.	1st Battalion, May 3, 1917, Ohsweken and Newport, Ontario.
Private	*MASASK-APEW	Charles	28th Battalion, August 9, 1918, Starblanket Band, Balcarres, Saskatchewan.
Private	McCORRISTER	Oswald	16th Battalion, February 15, 1918, Peguis Band, Hodgson, Manitoba.
Private	McCORRISTER	William R.	78th Battalion, June 26, 1919, Peguis Band, Hodgson, Manitoba.
Private	*McDONALD	Hugh John, MM	49th Battalion, February 12, 1919, the Yukon and Winnipeg, Manitoba.
Private	*McDONALD	Philip	8th Battalion, January 3, 1916, St. Regis Band, Cornwall, Ontario.
Private	*McGAHEY	Joseph Martin	54th Battalion, August 8, 1918, Caradoc, Ontario.
Sapper	*McWATCH	Jacob	4th Canadian Railway Transport, March 1, 1918, Chapleau, Ontario.
Private	*McWATCH	Simon	5th Pioneer Battalion, May 18, 1918, Chapleau, Ontario.
Private	MILLER	Huron Samuel	114th Battalion, November 12, 1916, Ohsweken, Ontario.
Private	*MISINISH-KOTEWE	Vincent	73rd Battalion, April 9, 1917, Manitowaning, Manitoulin Island, Ontario.
Private	*MITCHELL	Alexander	78th Battalion, April 9, 1917, Poplar River, Manitoba.
Private	*MITCHELL	Elias	18th Battalion, August 28, 1918, Saugeen Band, Chippawa Hill, Ontario.
Private	MONTOUR	William B.	4th Battalion, October 3, 1916, Hagersville, Ontario.
Private	*MOODY	Frank	1st Canadian Pioneer Battalion, October 8, 1916, Nass River, British Columbia.
Private	*MOORE	Gilbert	78th Battalion, March 24, 1918, Oak River Reserve, Griswold, Manitoba.

Lieutenant	*MOSES	James David	Royal Air Force, April 1, 1918, Ohsweken, Ontario.
Driver	*MOUNTAIN HORSE	Albert	1st Divisional Transport, November 19, 1915, Blood Reserve, Macleod, Alberta.
Private	MUNGO	Thomas	16th Battalion, August 17, 1917, Deseronto, Bay of Quinte, Ontario.
Private	*MURDOCK	Amos	1st Canadian Mounted Rifles, September 15, 1916, Fisher River Band, The Halfway, Manitoba.
Private	NACKOGIE	Bertie	228th Battalion, December 26, 1916, New Post Band, Moosonee, Ontario.
Private	NADJIWON	Paul	160th Battalion, January 15, 1917, Cape Croker, Ontario.
Sapper	NAHBEXIE	Austin	Canadian Railway Troops, June 6, 1920, White Bear Band, Carlyle, Saskatchewan.
Private	*NAWASH	Daniel	18th Battalion, August 27, 1918, Saugeen Band, Chippawa Hill, Ontario.
Sapper	NEWHOUSE	Elijah Levi	Canadian Engineers, March 5, 1921. Hagersville, Ontario.
Private	*NEWHOUSE	Henry Melvin	1st Battalion, June 21, 1917, Hagersville, Ontario.
Sapper	*NIGANIWINA	Thomas	1st Tramway Company, Canadian Engineers, August 20, 1918, Morrisville, Manitoulin Island, Ontario.
Private	NIGONAWAH	Eli Louis	227th Battalion, October 24, 1916, Sheshegwaning, Manitoulin Island, Ontario.
Private	*NOAH	Alexander Rufus	9th Battalion, Canadian Engineers, November 5, 1918, Chippewas of the Thames Band, Middlemiss and Muncey, Ontario.
Private	NOAH	Arthur Ebenezer	107th Pioneer Battalion, August 13, 1919, Thamesville, Ontario.
Private	NORTON	Louis Jacob	227th Battalion, August 28, 1916, West Bay, Manitoulin Island, Ontario.
Private	*NORWEST	Henry, MM	50th Battalion, August 18, 1918, Fort Saskatchewan and Buffalo Lake, Alberta.
Private	*ODJICK	Joseph	75th Battalion, September 21, 1918, Maniwaki, Quebec.
Private	OGEMAH	Grant	44th Battalion, September-December 1921, Shoal Lake Band, Shoal Lake, Ontario.
Private	*OUILLETTE	Peter	78th Battalion, October 30, 1917, St. Claude, Manitoba.
Private	PAINTED NOSE	Francois	243rd Battalion, 1918, One Arrow Band, Batoche, Saskatchewan.
Private	*PAQUETTE	Thomas	22nd Battalion, July 23, 1917, Odanak Band, Pierreville, Quebec.

Private	*PAUL	Joseph	16th Battalion, September 4-7, 1916, St. Eustache, Manitoba.
Private	*PAUL	Joseph Peter	2nd Pioneer Battalion, December 19, 1916, Big Cove Band, Rexton, New Brunswick.
Private	PAUL	Noel	Canadian Forestry Corps, January 11, 1919, Baddeck, Nova Scotia.
Private	*PEARSON	Daniel, MM	47th Battalion, October 15, 1917, Metlakatla Band, Prince Rupert, British Columbia.
Private	*PELTIER	Andrew	52nd Battalion, July 4, 1917, Manitoulin Island, Ontario.
Private	*PETERS	Alexander	21st Battalion, December 16, 1917, Ohsweken, Ontario.
Private	PETERS	John	149th Battalion, August 20, 1916, Walpole Island Band, Wallaceburg, Ontario.
Private	*PETERS	Joseph	102nd Battalion, April 9, 1917, Standing Buffalo Band, Fort Qu'Appelle, Saskatchewan.
Private	*PICARD	Joseph	8th Battalion, July 2, 1916, Loretteville, Quebec.
Private	*PINNANCE	Judson	47th Battalion, September 28, 1918, Walpole Island Band, Wallaceburg, Ontario.
Private	POTTS	Roderick	3rd Labour Battalion, September 21, 1919, Bear Island and Chapleau, Ontario.
Lance Corporal	*PROVOST	Peter	43rd Battalion, August 16, 1918, Peigan Band, Brocket, Alberta.
Private	QUACHIGAN	Daniel	Canadian Forestry Corps, December 31, 1917, Moose Factory, James Bay, Ontario.
Private	*QUINNIE	Joseph	Canadian Army Service Corps, November 5, 1918, Saddle Lake, Alberta.
Private	RAZOR	Raymond	Canadian Forestry Corps, April 29, 1922, Keeseekoose Band, Kamsack, Saskatchewan.
Private	REDBREAST	Jacob	Canadian Forestry Corps, August 24, 1918, Brunswick Band, Chapleau, Ontario.
Private	*RICHARD	Roger Victor	52nd Battalion, October 4, 1918, St. Ambroise, Manitoba.
Private	*RIEL	Patrick	8th Battalion, January 14, 1916, Port Arthur, Ontario.
Private	*RITCHIE	Peter	18th Battalion, August 27, 1918, Saugeen Band, Chippawa Hill, Ontario.
Private	RUDLAND	John Edward	1st Pioneer Battalion, October 4, 1916, Nass River, British Columbia.

Private	*RYAN	Walter	1st Pioneer Battalion, July 7, 1916, Port Simpson Band, Port Simpson, British Columbia.
Private	RYDER	Henry	Depot Battalion (1st Central Ontario Regiment), October 20, 1918, Temagami Band, Bear Island, Ontario.
Sergeant	*SALMON	Robert S.	49th Battalion, June 2, 1916, Fort Smith, Alberta.
Private	SANDERSON	William	107th Pioneer Battalion, July 16, 1917, Winnipegosis, Manitoba.
Private	SANDS	Allen	47th Battalion, February 16, 1921, Walpole Island Band, Wallaceburg, Ontario.
Private	SANDY	Adam	114th Battalion, December 6, 1917, Ohsweken, Ontario.
Private	SAYER	Denis	Canadian Forestry Corps, February 18, 1921, Garden River Band, Garden River, Ontario.
Private	SCHUYLER	John Mitchell ('Jack')	4th Battalion, August 17, 1917, Oneidas of the Thames, Delaware Township, Ontario.
Private	*SCOTT	James Alvin	29th Battalion, April 9, 1917, New Westminister, British Columbia.
Private	*SERO	Reuben	Princess Patricia's Canadian Light Infantry, October 30, 1917, Bay of Quinte, Ontario.
Private	*SEVELL (SEWELL)	Xavier (F)	42nd Battalion, April 16, 1917, Restigouche Band, Bonaventure County, Restigouche, Quebec.
Private	*SEYMOUR	Noel	Canadian Forestry Corps, June 10, 1918, Seabird Island Band, Agassiz, British Columbia.
Sapper	SHAWAN (SHAWAN-AGEESIE)	Joseph	2nd Tramway Company, September 7, 1918, Cape Croker, Ontario.
Private	SHAWINE-GABO	Peter	227th Battalion, March 26, 1917, Nipigon and Chapleau, Ontario.
Private	SHILLING (served as HILL)	Arthur	19th Battalion, October 8, 1920, Rama Indian Band, Rama, Ontario.
Lance Corporal	*SHIWAK	John	Royal Newfoundland Regiment, November 20, 1917, Rigolet, Labrador.
Private	SIMPSON	Archie	87th Battalion, May 13, 1917, Alderville Band, Hastings, Ontario.
Corporal	SIMPSON	John	114th Battalion, May 16, 1920, Caughnawaga, Quebec.
Private	SINCLAIR	George C.	Fort Garry Horse, April 15, 1921, Peguis Band, Hodgson, Manitoba.
Private	*SINCLAIR	John George	43rd Battalion, April 5, 1917, Fisher River

			Band, The Halfway, Manitoba.
Private	*SINCLAIR	McIvor	1st Canadian Mounted Rifles, November 8, 1916, Fisher River Band, Koostatak, Manitoba.
Private	SISSENAH	Archie	227th Battalion, November 8, 1916, Spanish River Band, Massey, Ontario.
Private	*SMART	Harold	25th Battalion, September 29, 1916, Bay of Quinte, Ontario.
Private	SMITH	Benjamin	43rd Battalion, November 14, 1917, St. Peters Band, Selkirk, Manitoba.
Private	*SMITH	William M.	1st Battalion, June 27, 1917, Six Nations, Ohsweken, Ontario.
Private	*SPLICER	Angus	PPCLI, June 4, 1916, Iroquois of the Caughnawaga Band, Caughnawaga, Quebec.
Private	*SPRAGUE	Neil	38th Battalion, June 13, 1918, Oneidas of the Thames, St. Thomas, Ontario.
Sapper	STAATS	Frank	Canadian Railway Troops, 257th Battalion, March 5, 1917, Ohsweken, Ontario.
Lieutenant	*STACEY	John Randolph	Royal Air Force, April 8, 1918, Caughnawaga, Quebec.
Private	*STEVENSON	George James	43rd Battalion, August 8, 1918, St. Peters Band, Selkirk, Manitoba.
Lance Corporal	STEVENSON	William James, MM	1st Battalion, May 15, 1920, Alderville Band, Cobourg, Ontario.
Private	*ST-GERMAIN	Edmund	43rd Battalion, August 16, 1918, St. Norbert, Manitoba.
Private	*STOQUA	Michael Joseph	75th Battalion, April 12, 1917, Golden Lake, Ontario.
Private	*STRANGER	David William	1st Canadian Mounted Rifles, March 29, 1917, St. Peters Band, Selkirk, Manitoba.
Private	SUTHERLAND	Solomon	Canadian Forestry Corps, February 12, 1919, Attawapiskat Band, Attawapiskat, James Bay, Ontario.
Private	SUTHERLAND	Thomas	Canadian Forestry Corps, April 8, 1920, Attawapiskat Band, Attawapiskat, Ontario.
Private	SWANSON	Peter	Canadian Forestry Corps, August 8, 1919, Attawapiskat Band, Attawapiskat, James Bay, Ontario.
Private	TAYLOR	Isaac	18th Battalion, January 8, 1917, Scugog Band, Port Perry, Ontario.
Private	TAYLOR	John	8th Battalion, September 9, 1917, Oak River Band, Griswold, Manitoba.
Private	*TENISCO	Moses	107th Pioneer Battalion, June 27, 1917, Golden Lake, Ontario.

Private	*TENNISCO	Alexander	38th Battalion, April 24, 1918, Golden Lake, Ontario.
Private	*THOMAS	Charles A.	3rd Battalion, June 20, 1916, Ohsweken and Toronto, Ontario.
Private	*THOMAS	David	43rd Battalion, October 26, 1917, Peguis Band, The Halfway, Manitoba.
Private	THOMAS	Morgan	4th Reserve Battalion, March 6, 1918, Walpole Island, Ontario.
Private	*THOMAS	John	107th Pioneer Battalion, August 15, 1917, Peguis Band, The Halfway, Manitoba.
Private	*THOMPSON (served as RYAN)	Charles Thomas	13th Battalion, July 16, 1916, Port Simpson Band, Port Simpson, British Columbia.
Private	*TOBIAS	Walter	123rd Canadian Pioneer Battalion, October 21, 1917, Moravians of the Thames Band, Moraviantown, Ontario.
Private	*TOBICO	Robert	19th Battalion, August 15, 1917, Alderville Band, Roseneath, Ontario.
Private	*TOBICOE	Maxwell	18th Battalion, November 9, 1917, Hagersville and New Credit, Ontario.
Private	*TOMER	Stephen	Canadian Army Veterinary Corps, April 6, 1918, Woodstock Band, Woodstock, New Brunswick.
Private	*TONEY	Louis	44th Battalion, September 28, 1918, Lennox Island, Prince Edward Island.
Private	*TRADER	Robert	52nd Battalion, October 29, 1917, Manitou Rapids Band, Barwick, Ontario.
Private	*TRONSON	James	47th Battalion, October 26, 1917, Okanagan Band, Vernon, British Columbia.
Private	*TURNER	Edgar Douglas	24th Battalion, November 6, 1917, Chapleau, Ontario.
Private	*TURNER	John Edward	52nd Battalion, June 18, 1917, Chapleau, Ontario.
Private	*VAN EVERY	Frederick	2nd Battalion, September 10, 1918, Hagersville, Ontario.
Private	*VICAIRE	John	26th Battalion, December 30, 1915, Maria Band, Dimock Creek, Quebec.
Private	*VIVIER	Alexander	1st Canadian Mounted Rifles, September 29, 1918, Marquette, Manitoba.
Sapper	*VYSE	James E.	11th Battalion, Canadian Engineers, October 23, 1918, Ohsweken, Ontario.
Private	*WABANOSSE	Michael	52nd Battalion, August 26, 1917, Manitowaning, Manitoulin Island, Ontario.
Private	*WALKER	Frank	12th Reserve Battalion, October 26, 1918, Ohsweken, Ontario.

Private	WARNER	Albert	161st Battalion, October 15, 1917, Walpole Island Band, Wallaceburg, Ontario.
Private	*WESLEY	Thomas Alexander	16th Battalion, August 16, 1917, St. Peters Band, Selkirk, Manitoba.
Private	*WHISKEY	St. James	8th Battalion, August 15, 1917, Cross Lake Band, Cross Lake, Manitoba.
Sapper	*WILSON	Lewis	Canadian Engineers, August 31, 1918, Ohsweken, Ontario.
Private	*WILSON	Simon	107th Pioneer Battalion, August 17, 1917, Hagersville, Ontario.
Private	*WHITE	Daniel K.	47th Battalion, August 12, 1918, Walpole Island Band, Wallaceburg, Ontario.
Private	*WHITE	Louis	5th Battalion, September 1, 1918, Sweetgrass Band, Battleford, Saskatchewan.
Private	*WHITE	Phillip	1st Battalion, August 30, 1918, St. Regis Band, Cornwall, Ontario.
Private	YELLOW	Newton	107th Pioneer Battalion, February 20, 1918, Ohsweken, Ontario.
Private	YOUNG	Albert	197th Battalion, January 12, 1917, The Pas, Manitoba.

ADDENDA
First World War

Some veterans whose deaths (1919-1922) were not directly attributed to war service.

BAPTISTE	Joseph John	December 17, 1919, Maniwaki, Quebec.
BELL	John	119th Battalion, October 1921, Sheshegwaning Band, Sheshegwaning, Manitoulin Island, Ontario.
COOK	Robert	Canadian Forestry Corps, December 29, 1919, The Pas, Manitoba.
COTE	Edward	June 5, 1922, Cote Band, Kamsack, Saskatchewan.
DOWAN	Samuel	43rd Battalion, Oak River Reserve, Griswold, Manitoba.
ENOSSE	Joseph P.	April 15, 1920, Wikwemikong, Manitowaning, Ontario.
FRANCIS	Noel	May 1923, Sydney Band, Sydney, Nova Scotia.
FRANCOIS	Abel	172nd Battalion, January 11, 1920, Chase, British Columbia.
GLODE	James A.	August 5, 1922, Millbrook, Nova Scotia.
HEAD	Walter	November 6, 1919, The Pas, Manitoba.
LABOBE	Peter	Canadian Railway Transport, Lennox Island, Prince Edward Island.

McDOUGALL	Jacko	July 20, 1922, Maniwaki, Quebec.
NAWASH	David	160th Battalion, October 12, 1918, Chippawa Hill, Ontario.
PETERS	Jacob	February 4, 1922, Lennox Island, Prince Edward Island.
PIERRISH	Francois	Canadian Forestry Corps, November 4, 1921, Neskainlith Band, Shuswap, British Columbia.
RAZER	Graham	April 24, 1922, 107th Battalion, Keeseekoose Band, Kamsack, Saskatchewan.
SAPPIER	Joseph	Eel River Band, Newcastle, New Brunswick.
SANDERSON	William B.	28th Battalion, 1921, Muskeg Lake Band, Aldina, Saskatchewan.
SEWATIS	Alex	80th Battalion, St. Regis, Cornwall, Ontario.
SILVERSMITH	C.	May 22, 1923, Ohsweken, Ontario.
STONEFISH	George	February 14, 1920, Moravians of the Thames Band, Bothwell, Ontario.
TAYLOR	Alexander	160th Battalion, August 12, 1920, Cape Croker, Ontario.

APPENDIX C

Honours and Awards
First World War, 1914-1918

				Award
Private	AKIWENZIE	Charles	43rd Battalion, Cape Croker, Ontario.	MM
Private	ANDERSON	Andrew William	107th Battalion, Fort Qu'Appelle (Punnichy), Saskatchewan.	MM
Private	BELANGER	Augustin	52nd Battalion, Fort William, Ontario.	MM
Sergeant	BOUCHARD	Leo	52nd Battalion, Lake Nipigon, Ontario.	DCM
Private	CLEARY	Willie	22nd Battalion, Lac St. Jean, Quebec.	MM
Private	COOK	Edwin Victor	7th Battalion, Alert Bay, British Columbia.	DCM
Private	DeLARONDE	Joseph	52nd Battalion, Nipigon, Ontario.	MM
Corporal	DREAVER	Joseph	3rd Battalion,Canadian Engineers, Mistawasis Band, Leask, Saskatchewan.	MM
Private	FAITHFUL	David	47th Battalion, Port Simpson Band, Port Simpson, British Columbia.	MM
Corporal	GLODE	Samuel	6th Battalion, Canadian Engineers, Milton, Nova Scotia	DCM
Private	GODCHERE	Thomas	102nd Battalion, Long Lake Band, Longlac, Ontario.	MM
Private	HAPA	Herbert	52nd Battalion, Sioux Valley Band, Manitoba.	MM
Bombardier	HILL	Joseph Bernard	Canadian Field Artillery, Bay of Quinte, Ontario.	MM
Sapper	KEEPER	Joseph B.	1st Battalio, Canadian	

				Engineers, Norway House, Manitoba.	MM
Private	KISEK (KEJICK)	David		52nd Battalion, Shoal Lake, Ontario.	DCM
Private	McDONALD	Hugh John		49th Battalion, the Yukon and Winnipeg, Manitoba.	MM
Private	McLEAN	George		54th Battalion, Douglas Lake, British Columbia.	DCM
Private	MISINISH-KOTEWE	Francis		73rd Battalion, Manitoulin Island, Ontario.	Cross of the Order of Saint George, 4th Class.
Private	NORWEST	Henry		50th Battalion, Fort Saskatchewan, Alberta.	MM and Bar
Lance Corporal	PAUDASH	Johnson		21st Battalion, Hiawatha Band, Keene, Ontario.	MM
Private	PEARSON	Daniel		47th Battalion, Metlakatala Band, Prince Rupert, British Columbia.	MM
Corporal	PEGAHM-AGABOW	Francis		1st Battalion, Parry Sound, Ontario.	MM and two Bars.
Private	ROUSSIN	Joseph		22nd Battalion, Oka, Quebec.	MM
Private	SANDERSON	N.G.		5th Battalion, Lily Plain (Leask), Saskatchewan.	MM
Private	SIMCOE	Ben		19th Battalion, Orillia, Ontario.	MM
Lieutenant	SMITH	A.G.E.		20th Battalion, Ohsweken, Ontario.	MC
Lance Corporal	STEVENSON	William James		4th Battalion, Alderville, Ontario.	MM
Driver	THEBERGE	Delphis		9th Brigade, Canadian Field Artillery, Lorette, Quebec.	MM
Private	WILLIAMS	Enos		1st Battalion, Ohsweken, Ontario.	MM
Private	YAHBA	John Henry		18th Battalion, Saugeen Band, Chippawa Hill, Ontario.	DCM

APPENDIX D

ROLL OF HONOUR

(*Killed in Action or Died of Wounds or Accident Overseas from War Service)

Second World War, 1939 -1945

Private	*ABRAHAM	Emile	Queen's Own Cameron Highlanders of Canada, July 22, 1944, Long Lake Band, Longlac, Ontario.
Private	*ADAMS	Clarence	Royal Canadian Infantry Corps, December 19, 1944, Carry the Kettle Band, Sintaluta, Saskatchewan.
Lance Corporal	*ALEXIS	Alexander	Royal Winnipeg Rifles, August 18, 1944, Tache Band, Fort St. James, British Columbia.
Private	*ASHKEWE	Benjamin Roy	Queen's Own Cameron Highlanders of Canada, November 29, 1944, Cape Croker, Ontario.
Private	*BADGER	George Charles	Winnipeg Grenadiers, November 5, 1943, Cote Band, Kamsack, Saskatchewan.
Private	*BALDHEAD	James Luke	South Saskatchewan Regiment, July 20, 1944, One Arrow Band, Batoche, Saskatchewan.
Private	*BAPTISTE	Edgar Herbert	Winnipeg Grenadiers, December 19, 1941, Red Pheasant Reserve, Battleford, Saskatchewan.
Private	*BARNHARDT	Carman Francis	Black Watch (Royal Highland Regt.) of Canada, July 25, 1944, Caledonia, Ontario.
Private	*BARRON	Oliver Amy	Winnipeg Grenadiers, December 19, 1941, St. Laurent, Manitoba.
Trooper	*BEESWAX	William Alvin	Governor General's Horse Guards, October 27, 1944, Munceys of the Thames Band, Melbourne, Ontario.
Fusilier	*BEAR	Thomas	Princess Louise Fusiliers, January 13, 1945, Meadow Lake Band, Meadow Lake, Saskatchewan.
Gunner	*BEARDY	Rose	Royal Canadian Artillery, July 30, 1944, Cross Lake, Manitoba.
Rifleman	*BEAVER	Arthur William	Queen's Own Rifles of Canada, October

			1, 1944, Alderville Band, Cobourg, Ontario.
Rifleman	*BEAUREG- ARD	Wilfred Joseph	Regina Rifles, June 9, 1944, St. Paul, Alberta.
Rifleman	*BELLEGARDE	Maurice	Regina Rifles, November 3, 1944, Peepeekisis Band, File Hills, Abernethy, Saskatchewan.
Lance Corporal	*BERNARD	Matthew	Royal Canadian Army Service Corps, March 23, 1944, Eel River Band, New Brunswick.
Private	BIG CANOE	Thomas Beresford	Royal Hamilton Light Infantry, March 8, 1945, Georgina Island, Ontario.
Sapper	BOY	Frank	Royal Canadian Engineers, June 18, 1946, Seine River Band, Mine Centre near Fort Frances, Ontario.
Private	BRANT	Clifford Lloyd	Argyll and Sutherland Highlanders of Canada, April 25, 1941, Hamilton, Ontario.
Private	*BRANT	Elmer Joseph	Royal Hamilton Light Infantry, August 19, 1942, Deseronto, Ontario.
Private	*BRANT	Huron Eldon, MM	Hastings and Prince Edward Regiment, October 14, 1944, Deseronto, Ontario.
Private	*BRANT	Jacob Shelby	Lincoln and Welland Regiment, September 11, 1944, Hagersville, Ontario.
Private	*BRANT	Jerry	Seaforth Highlanders of Canada, May 24, 1944, Bay of Quinte, Ontario.
Private	*BRANT	Kenneth	Hastings and Prince Edward Regiment, January 31, 1944, Tyendinaga Reserve, Deseronto, Ontario.
Private	*BRANT	Lloyd Edwin	Hastings and Prince Edward Regiment, December 14, 1943, Deseronto, Ontario.
Rifleman	*BRESSETTE	Lloyd Henry	Queen's Own Rifles of Canada, July 18, 1944, Kettle Point Band, Forest, Ontario.
Private	*BROOKS	Louis Peter	Royal Canadian Regiment, May 30, 1944, Shubenacadie Band, Hants County, Nova Scotia.
Lieutenant	*BROSSEAU	Albert Edmond	Le Regiment de Maisonneuve, July 28, 1944, St. Paul, Alberta.
Gunner	BROWN	Isaac	Royal Canadian Artillery, September 6, 1943, Babine Band, Babine, British Columbia.
Private	*BROWNLEE	John	Lake Superior Regiment, November 8, 1944, Wabigoon Band, Dinorwic, Ontario.
Private	*BRYANT	William John	Queen's Own Cameron Highlanders of Canada, August 28, 1944, Cote Band, Kamsack, Saskatchewan.
Private	*BURNHAM	Ellwood Martin	47th Infantry Regiment (U.S.), March 19, 1945, Ohsweken, Ontario.

Corporal (A/Sgt)	*CAMPION	George Alexander MM	Loyal Edmonton Regiment, May 23, 1944, Tofield, Alberta.
Private	*CANTIN	Robert	Lake Superior Regiment, August 28, 1944, Wabigoon Band, Dinorwic, Ontario.
Flight Sergeant	*CAPTON	Leslie James	RCAF, No. 49 (RAF) Squadron, August 29, 1942, Ohsweken, Ontario.
Private	*CARDINAL	Solomon	Loyal Edmonton Regiment, September 18, 1944, Goodfish Lake, Alberta.
Trooper	*CARRIERE	Florio	British Columbia Dragoons, May 29, 1944, St. Pierre, Manitoba.
Private	*CARRIERE	Frederic	Essex Scottish, October 26, 1944, St. Eustache, Manitoba.
Private	*CHABOYER	David	Winnipeg Grenadiers, March 13, 1945, St. Laurent, Manitoba.
Flying Officer	*CHAPPISE	Richard	RCAF, No. 99 (RAF) Squadron, June 5, 1945, Chapleau, Ontario.
Private	*CHARTRAND	Adelard Joseph	Lake Superior Regiment, March 9, 1945, Camperville, Manitoba.
Lance Sergeant	*CHARTRAND	Lawrence	Royal Winnipeg Rifles, June 8, 1944, Camperville, Manitoba.
Gunner	CHARTERS	Henry Patrick	Royal Canadian Artillery, July 4, 1941, Merritt, British Columbia.
Rifleman	*CHASKE	Tom	Royal Winnipeg Rifles, December 12, 1944, Long Plain Band, Edwin, Manitoba.
Private	*CHIPPEWA	Donald Wellington	Algonquin Regiment, August 10, 1944, Caldwell Band, Essex, Ontario.
Sergeant	*CHUBB	Wilburn	Irish Regiment of Canada, February 2, 1944, Alderville Band, Roseneath, Ontario.
Private	*CLUTESI	Edward John	Calgary Highlanders, August 29, 1944, Opetchesaht Band, Port Alberni, British Columbia.
Private	*CONTIN	Wilfred	Perth Regiment, December 8, 1944, Henvey Inlet Band, Pickerel, Ontario.
Lance Corporal	*COOK	Edwin Victor	Calgary Highlanders, September 30, 1944, Nimpkish Band, Alert Bay, British Columbia.
Private	*COPE	Leo	North Nova Scotia Highlanders, June 9, 1944, Truro Band, Nova Scotia.
Bombardier	CRATE	Leonard Victor	Royal Canadian Artillery, January 5, 1945, Fisher River Band, Koostatak, Manitoba.
Sapper	*CULBERT-SON	John	Royal Canadian Engineers, April 30, 1945, Belleville, Ontario.
Lance Corporal	*DAIGNE-AULT	John	Regina Rifles, October 6, 1944, St. Paul, Alberta.

Rifleman	*DANIELS	William	Royal Winnipeg Rifles, April 22, 1945, Big River Band, Victoire, Saskatchewan.
Private	*DEER	Harold	U.S. Army, February 8, 1945, Caughnawaga Band, Caughnawaga, Quebec.
Private	*DESNOMIE	Joseph Noel	The Black Watch (Royal Highland Regiment) of Canada, September 29, 1944, Peepeekisis Band, Lorlie, Saskatchewan.
Private	DICK	Clarence George	Royal Canadian Army Service Corps, February 3, 1945, Songhees Band, Victoria, British Columbia.
Private	DICK	Daniel	Royal Canadian Infantry Corps, April 30, 1945, Fort William Band, Ontario.
Lance Corporal	DOMINIC	Reginald Daniel	Royal Canadian Army Service Corps, July 30, 1945, Burrard Band, (Seymour Heights) North Vancouver, British Columbia.
Sergeant	*DREAVER	Harvey	Regina Rifles, October 6, 1944, Mistawasis Band, Leask, Saskatchewan.
Private	*DUCHARME	John Clifford	South Saskatchewan Regiment, July 23, 1944, Keg River, Alberta.
Trooper	*DUMONT	John	1st Hussars (6th Armoured Regiment) June 11, 1944, Peepeekisis Band, Lorlie, Saskatchewan.
Private	*ELM	Leslie	Canadian Scottish, August 16, 1944, Oneidas of the Thames, Southwold, Ontario.
Private	*EYAHPAISE	Edward Stanley	Queen's Own Cameron Highlanders of Canada, July 21, 1944, Beardy Band, Duck Lake, Saskatchewan.
Rifleman	*FAGNAN	Anthony Alec	Royal Winnipeg Rifles, June 8, 1944, Camperville, Manitoba.
Private	*FLAMAND	Frederick	South Saskatchewan Regiment, August 8, 1944, Camperville, Manitoba.
Trooper	*FLETT	Alfred James	12th Manitoba Dragoons (18th Armoured Car Regiment) Stony Point, Manitoba, February 8, 1945.
Gunner	FRANCIS	George	Royal Canadian Artillery, January 7, 1945, Lennox Island, Prince Edward Island.
Private	*GARNEAU	Daniel	Princess Patricia's Canadian Light Infantry, July 22, 1943, Wabigoon Band, Dinorwic, Ontario.
Lance Sergeant	*GENAILLE	John Henry	Lake Superior Regiment, August 12, 1944, Shortdale, Manitoba.
Corporal	*GEORGE	Ernest Baptiste	Lanark and Renfrew Scottish Regiment, December 13, 1944, Osoyoos Band, Oliver and Inkaneep, British Columbia.
Private	GEORGE (CORNELIUS)	Wilfred	Highland Light Infantry of Canada, February 16, 1947, Oneidas of the

			Thames, Muncey, Ontario.
Private	*GILROY	Wilbert Norman	Stormont, Dundas and Glengarry Highlanders, July 8, 1944, Belleville, Ontario.
Private	*GOULAIS	Michael Clarence	Royal Hamilton Light Infantry, August 19, 1942, Nipissing Band, Sturgeon Falls, Ontario.
Lance Corporal	*GREEN	Howard Kenneth	Hastings and Prince Edward Regiment, May 22, 1944, Bay of Quinte, Ontario.
Private	*GREEN	Kenneth Robert	Hastings and Prince Edward Regiment, July 26, 1944, Chapleau, Ontario.
Lance Bombardier	*GREEN	Russell Raymond	Royal Canadian Artillery, August 13, 1944, Tyendinaga Reserve, resided at Sarnia, Ontario.
Private	*GRINDER	James Edward	Seaforth Highlanders of Canada, December 14, 1944, Big Bar Creek, British Columbia.
Rifleman	*GUIBOCHE	Lawrence Roderick	Royal Winnipeg Rifles, June 8, 1944, Camperville, Manitoba.
Private	HALL	John	Royal Canadian Ordnance Corps, January 16, 1945, Caughnawaga Band, Caughnawaga, Quebec.
Private	*HALLER	Alvin	North Nova Scotia Highlanders, September 17, 1944, Douglas Lake, British Columbia.
Private	HAMILTON	George	Canadian Scottish, January 5, 1945, Alberni, British Columbia.
Private	*HENRY	Joseph	Algonquin Regiment, October 20, 1944, Roseau River Band, Letellier, Manitoba.
Private	*HENRY	Joseph E.	U.S. Army, May 12, 1945, Hagersville, Ontario.
Private	*HENRY	Norman Walter	Royal Hamilton Light Infantry, August 19, 1942, Hagersville, Ontario.
Private	*HILL	George Leonard	Essex Scottish, August 26, 1944, Six Nations, Cainsville, Ontario.
Gunner	*HOULE	Simon	Royal Canadian Artillery, October 1, 1944, Saddle Lake, Alberta.
Gunner	*HUNTER	James	Royal Canadian Artillery, December 26, 1944, Hunters-Point, Quebec.
Private	*HUTCH	Wifred Jack	Canadian Scottish, June 9, 1944, Williams Lake, British Columbia.
Private	*IRONS	George Bradley	48th Highlanders of Canada, April 13, 1945, Curve Lake near Peterborough, Ontario.
Acting Corporal	*JAMIESON	Harold	Queen's Own Rifles of Canada, April 2, 1945, Ohsweken, Ontario.
Private	*JARDINE	Albert	Loyal Edmonton Regiment, December 30,

			1943, Stellaquo Band, Fraser Lake, British Columbia.
Private	JASPER	David William	Westminster Regiment, October 9, 1941, Lakahahmen Band, Deroche, British Columbia.
WO2	*JEFFRIES	Samuel	No. 104 (RAF) Squadron, December 28, 1942, Missanabie, Ontario.
Private	JOHN	David Elliott	Royal Canadian Ordnance Corps, October 1, 1944, Ohsweken, Ontario.
Private	*JOHN	Maurice	Royal Canadian Regiment, May 16, 1944, Saugeen Band, Chippawa Hill, Ontario.
Private	*JOHNNY	Augustine	The Black Watch (Royal Highland Regiment) of Canada, July 25, 1944, Williams Lake Band, Williams Lake, British Columbia.
Gunner	JOHNSON	Richard	Royal Canadian Artillery, July 2, 1944, Teslin Lake Band, Teslin Lake and Carcross, Yukon.
Private	*JONES	Stanley Owen	Canadian Scottish Regiment, September 8, 1945, Masset Band, Masset, British Columbia.
Trooper	KAKAWAY	Albert	16th/22nd Saskatchewan Horse, October 11, 1942, Cote Band, Kamsack, Saskatchewan.
Private	*KAVANA-UGH	Robert Leo	Regina Rifles, July 19, 1944, Rainy River Band, Emo, Ontario.
Private	*KEEWATIN	Maurice William	South Saskatchewan Regiment, August 28, 1944, Peepeekisis Band, Balcarres, Saskatchewan.
Private	*KING	Maxwell Jacob	Royal Hamilton Light Infantry, August 19, 1942, Hagersville, Ontario.
Private	KISHIGWEB	John	Princess Patricia's Canadian Light Infantry, March 2, 1946, Kashabowie and Fort William, Ontario.
Trooper	*KIT-CHEMONIA	Russell John	Fort Garry Horse, October 12, 1944, Kamsack, Saskatchewan.
Sergeant	*LALONDE	Gerald Grenville	No. 420 (RCAF) Squadron, April 19, 1942, Nipissing Band, Sturgeon Falls, Ontario.
Private	*LARUE	Robert Louis	Princess Patricia's Canadian Light Infantry, October 20, 1944, Kamloops Band, Kamloops, British Columbia.
Private	*LAVALEE	Ernest	Winnipeg Grenadiers, February 27, 1944, St. Laurent, Manitoba.
Private	LAVIGNE	John Henry	Royal Canadian Army Medical Corps, August 21, 1945, Restigouche Band, Restigouche, Quebec.
Private	*LEON	Charles	Seaforth Highlanders of Canada, July 21, 1943, Adams Lake Band, Chase, British Columbia.

Private	*LEONARD	Joseph Alan	Loyal Edmonton Regiment, December 29, 1944, Kamloops Band, Kamloops, British Columbia.
Private	*LESAGE	James A.	Royal Hamilton Light Infantry, August 1, 1944, Sault Ste. Marie, Ontario.
Private	*LETENDRE	Norman Joseph	Loyal Edmonton Regiment, April 12, 1945, Lac Ste. Anne, Alberta.
Private	*LEWIS	Walter Henry	Highland Light Infantry, March 24, 1945, Six Nations, Ohsweken, Ontario.
Sapper	*LITTLECROW	Harold Charles	Royal Canadian Engineers, July 26, 1944, Moose Woods Band, Dundurn, Saskatchewan.
Private	*LUCIE	Benjamin	The Black Watch (Royal Highland Regiment) of Canada, October 1, 1944, Glen Mary near Prince Albert, Saskatchewan.
Bombardier	*LUKE	William Andrew	Royal Canadian Artillery, March 7, 1945, Mattagami Band, Gogama, Ontario.
Rifleman	*LOUIS	Jean Baptiste	Royal Winnipeg Rifles, June 6, 1944, Fort William Band, Thunder Bay, Ontario.
Rifleman	*MANDAMIN	Henry Eugene	Royal Winnipeg Rifles, October 23, 1944, Kaboni, Manitoulin Island, Ontario.
Private	*MANY-WOUNDS	Teddy	Royal Canadian Army Service Corps, February 19, 1942, Sarcee Band, Calgary, Alberta.
Private	*MARACLE	Francis	Stormont, Dundas and Glengarry Highlanders, March 6, 1942, Bay of Quinte, Ontario.
Lance Sergeant	*MARTIN	Franklyn	Royal Hamilton Light Infantry, August 19, 1942, Six Nations, Oakland, Ontario.
Fusilier	*MARTINEAU	Edmund Peter Joseph	Princess Louise Fusiliers, May 22, 1944, Attawapiskat, Ontario.
Private	*McARTHUR	Daniel	South Saskatchewan Regiment, March 3, 1945, White Bear Band, (Moose Mountain) Carlyle, Saskatchewan.
Private	McARTHUR	Edward	South Saskatchewan Regiment, May 3, 1943, White Bear Band, (Moose Mountain) Carlyle, Saskatchewan.
Lance Corporal	*McGREGOR	Theodore	Essex Scottish, February 19, 1945, Whitefish River Band, Birch Island, Ontario.
Gunner	*McLEOD	Albert Alexander	Royal Canadian Artillery, June 19, 1945, Peepeekisis Band, Lorlie, Saskatchewan.
Private	*McLEOD	Alfred Joseph	Perth Regiment, January 17, 1944, Chippewas of Nawash, Wiarton, Ontario.
Gunner	*McLEOD	Edward Gilbert	Royal Canadian Artillery, February 26, 1945, Grouard, Alberta.
Trooper	*McLEOD	John Joseph	1st Hussars, (6th Armoured Regiment) Ju-

			ly 27, 1944, Chippewas of Nawash, Wiarton, Ontario.
Rifleman	*McPHERSON	Rudolph	Royal Winnipeg Rifles, September 27, 1944, Couchiching Band, Fort Frances, Ontario.
Rifleman	*MERCER	Stanley Jones	Royal Winnipeg Rifles, August 18, 1944, Wabowden, Manitoba.
Private	*MIKE	Sebastian	Calgary Highlanders, October 23, 1944, Tobacco Plains Band, Grasmere, British Columbia.
Corporal	*MONTOUR	Edward	U.S. Army, September 26, 1944, Caughnawaga Band, Caughnawaga, Quebec.
Private	*MONTOUR	Peter	U.S. Army, July 15, 1944, Caughnawaga, Band, Caughnawaga, Quebec.
Private	MOON	John	Prince Albert Volunteers, September 11, 1943, Comox, British Columbia.
Private	*MOORE	Bertrand Cyril	Winnipeg Grenadiers, July 15, 1945, Moose Factory, Ontario.
Able Seaman	*MOORE	Lloyd George	Royal Canadian Naval Volunteer Reserve (HMCS *St. Croix),* September 20, 1943, Regina, Saskatchewan.
Private	MORIN	Felix	South Saskatchewan Regiment, July 4, 1946, Big River Band, Pascal, Saskatchewan.
Private	*MORRIS	Frederick Earl	Queen's Own Cameron Highlanders of Canada, April 30, 1941, Punnichy, Saskatchewan. Drowned when *SS Nerissa* was torpedoed.
Private	MORRISSEAU	Edward Joseph	Winnipeg Grenadiers, December 23, 1945, Fort Alexander Band, Pine Falls, Manitoba.
Gunner	MURDOCK	Arthur	Royal Canadian Artillery, August 27, 1945, Fisher River Band, Koostatak, Manitoba.
Private	*MUSQUASH	Peter	Princess Patricia's Canadian Light Infantry, January 12, 1945, Pays Plat Band, Nipigon, Ontario.
Gunner	MUSWAGON	John Angus	Royal Canadian Artillery, September 13, 1944, Norway House, Manitoba.
Sapper	*MUT-CHEGUIS	Frank	Royal Canadian Engineers, July 28, 1944, Brunswick House Band, Peterbell, Ontario.
Rifleman	*NABISH	Wilfred Joseph	Royal Winnipeg Rifles, June 6, 1944, Eagle Lake Band, near Dryden, Ontario.
Private	*NADJIWAN	Francis Boniface	4th Princess Louise Dragoon Guards, September 13, 1944, Cape Croker, Ontario.
Rifleman	*NAHWEG-EZHIC	Charles, MM	Queen's Own Rifles of Canada, February 28, 1945, Sheguiandah,

			Manitoulin Island, Ontario.
Private	*NAHWEG EZHIC	Ronald	Hastings and Prince Edward Regiment, October 12, 1944, Sheguiandah, Manitoulin Island, Ontario.
Private	*NAMAYPOKE	Eddie	Lorne Scots (Peel, Dufferin and Halton Regiment), December 13, 1944, Manitou Rapids Band, Emo, Ontario.
Lance Corporal	*NANIBUSH	Charles	Algonquin Regiment, March 8, 1945, Shawanaga Band, near Nobel, Ontario.
Trooper	*NAWASH	Stafford David	Fort Garry Horse, August 10, 1944, Chippawa Hill, Ontario.
Private	*NICHOLAS	Paul Peter	Carleton and York Regiment, May 23, 1944, Tobique Band, Maliseet, New Brunswick.
Private	*NICHOLAS	Toby	Seaforth Highlanders of Canada, July 21, 1943, Columbia Lake Band, Windermere, British Columbia.
Rifleman	*NOKUSIS	Maurice Edward	Regina Rifles, July 8, 1944, Okanese Band, Lorlie, Saskatchewan.
Private	*NORRIS	Russell John	Calgary Highlanders, July 25, 1944, Fort Vermilion, Alberta.
Private	*NOSKEYI	Benjamin Joseph	Calgary Highlanders, August 23, 1944, Peace River, Alberta and Loon Lake, Saskatchewan.
Private	*OBEDIAH	Wilfred	North Nova Scotia Highlanders, July 8, 1944, Otterville, Ontario.
Private	*ODJICK	Basil Alias	Royal Regiment of Canada, August 28, 1944, Maniwaki, Quebec.
Private	*ODJICK	Robert Simon	Royal Regiment of Canada, April 17, 1944, Maniwaki, Quebec.
Private	*OKEMASIS	Joseph	Saskatoon Light Infantry, December 7, 1943, Muskeg Lake Band, Leask, Saskatchewan.
Private	*OSAWO- MICK	John	Royal Regiment of Canada, September 24, 1944, Kaboni, Manitoulin Island, Ontario.
Private	OUSTAN	Frederick	Royal Canadian Infantry Corps, January 25, 1945, Moose Factory, Ontario.
Rifleman	*PANGMAN	William	Royal Winnipeg Rifles, June 6, 1944, Duck Bay, Manitoba.
Rifleman	*PARISIAN	Percy	Royal Winnipeg Rifles, June 8, 1944, Peguis Band, Hodgson, Manitoba.
Private	*PARISIAN	Sydney	Queen's Own Cameron Highlanders of Canada, October 2, 1944, Peguis Band, Selkirk, Manitoba.
Private	*PATTERSON	Welby Lloyd, MM	Argyll and Sutherland Highlanders of Canada, April 14, 1945, Ohsweken, Ontario.

Flight Sergeant	PAUDASH	Elmer Robert	No. 115 (RAF) Squadron, September 21, 1942, Hiawatha Band, Keene, Ontario.
Private	*PAUL	Louis Gerald	Royal Regiment of Canada, August 24, 1944, Tobique Band, Maliseet, New Brunswick.
Private	*PEARSON	John	The Algonquin Regiment, July 30, 1944, Oneida of the Thames, Southwold, Ontario.
Private	*PEDONI QUOTT	Isadore	4th Princess Louise Dragoon Guards, September 23, 1944, Cape Croker, Ontario
Private	PHILLIPS	Adrian Joseph	Royal Canadian Army Service Corps, December 8, 1945, Skookumchuck Band Mission, British Columbia.
Private	*PICTOU	Francis	Carleton and York Regiment, September 12, 1944, Eel River Band, Darlington, New Brunswick.
Gunner	PIERRWAY	Alfred	Royal Canadian Artillery, July 12, 1942, Quesnel, British Columbia.
Private	*PINE	William Johan	Royal Regiment of Canada, July 27, 1944, Garden River Band, Echo Bay, Ontario.
Rifleman	*PITWAN AKWAT	Alfred Louis	Royal Winnipeg Rifles, February 21, 1945, Stoney Band, Morley, Alberta.
Private	*POITRAS	Edward Joseph	South Saskatchewan Regiment, August 19, 1942, Fort Qu'Appelle, Saskatchewan.
Rifleman	*PORTER	Joseph Nicholas	Royal Winnipeg Rifles, June 9, 1944, Camperville, Manitoba.
Rifleman	*POUCETTE	Joe	Royal Winnipeg Rifles, August 15, 1944, Stoney Band, Morley, Alberta.
Private	*POWLESS	Randall Arthur	U.S. Army, January 3, 1945, Hagersville, Ontario.
Rifleman	*PRATT	Kenneth Wilfred	Royal Winnipeg Rifles, June 7, 1944, Gordon Band, Punnichy, Saskatchewan.
Private	*PRINCE	Herbert	Princess Patricia's Canadian Light Infantry, February 3, 1945, Necoslie Band, Fort St. James, British Columbia.
Sapper	QUACHEGAN	William David	Royal Canadian Engineers, October 24, 1947, Moose Factory, Ontario.
Private	*RICE	Leonard	U.S. Army, January 19, 1943, Caughnawaga Band, Caughnawaga, Quebec.
Rifleman	*RIEL	Roland David	Regina Rifles, October 15, 1944, St. Vital, Manitoba.
Private	*RILEY	Lloyd Joseph	Calgary Highlanders, September 22, 1944, Chippewas of the Thames, Muncey, Ontario.
Private	ROSS	Roman	Veterans' Guard of Canada, February 20, 1946, Lorlie, Saskatchewan.

Trooper	*RYAN	Thomas Henry	1st Hussars, August 14, 1944, Port Simpson Band, Port Simpson, British Columbia.
Rifleman	*SABISTON	David Hamilton	Royal Winnipeg Rifles, June 12, 1944, Bankend, Saskatchewan.
Corporal	*SABISTON	William Wallace George	Royal Winnipeg Rifles, June 12, 1944, Bankend, Saskatchewan.
Sapper	SACK	Daniel	Royal Canadian Engineers, March 25, 1945, Moose Factory, James Bay, Ontario.
Private	*SACOBIE	Richard Garbil	Carleton and York Regiment, August 29, 1944, Oromocto Band, Oromocto, New Brunswick.
Private	*SADDLEMAN	Albert Joseph	Princess Patricia's Canadian Light Infantry, September 17, 1944, Okanagan Band, Vernon, British Columbia.
Lance Sergeant	*ST. GERMAIN	Joseph Flavien	Loyal Edmonton Regiment, December 14, 1944, Dixonville, Alberta.
Private	*ST. GERMAIN	Charles William	South Saskatchewan Regiment, September 16, 1944, Rama Band, Rama, Ontario.
Gunner	SAM	Peter Martin	Royal Canadian Artillery, April 21, 1941, Shuswap Band, Athalmer, British Columbia.
Private	SANDERSON	Isaac	Winnipeg Grenadiers, February 14, 1946, Selkirk, Manitoba.
Private	*SANDS	Roslyn Ernest	Essex Scottish, April 14, 1945, Walpole Island Band, Wallaceburg, Ontario.
Sapper	*SARK	James Linus	Royal Canadian Engineers, June 3, 1944, Lennox Island Band, Tracadie Cross, Prince Edward Island.
Sapper	*SAULIS	Sanford Steven	Royal Canadian Engineers, August 10, 1945, Tobique Band, Maliseet, New Brunswick.
Rifleman	*SAWDO	Louis	Royal Winnipeg Rifles, June 17, 1944, Savanne, Ontario.
Private	*SCRIBE	Kenneth	Highland Light Infantry, October 11, 1944, Norway House Band, Norway House, Manitoba.
Fusilier	*SETTEE	Alexander	11th Independent Machine Gun Company (Princess Louise Fusiliers), September 3, 1944, Cumberland House Band, Saskatchewan.
Private	SEYMOUR	Jacob	Hastings and Prince Edward Regiment, September 11, 1942, St. Regis Band, Cornwall, Ontario,
Private	*SHAWANDA	Isaac	Essex Scottish, July 31, 1944, Kaboni, Manitoulin Island, Ontario.
Private	*SHIPMAN	Willard Harris	Highland Light Infantry of Canada, July 8, 1944, Walpole Island, Ontario.

Private	*SIMPSON	Clarence	North Shore (New Brunswick Regiment), July 8, 1944, Okanagan Band, Vernon, British Columbia.
Private	*SINCLAIR	Joseph William	Royal Canadian Army Service Corps, August 14, 1944, Pikwitonei, Split Lake, Manitoba.
Private	SIOUI	Rosaire	Les Fusiliers Mont-Royal, July 14, 1943, Village Huron, Loretteville, Quebec.
Private	*SIOUX	Jean Joseph Anthony	Winnipeg Grenadiers, November 16, 1942, St. Laurent, Manitoba.
Private	*SKEAD	Frederick A.	Essex Scottish, February 19, 1945, Rat Portage Band, Kenora, Ontario.
Private	*SMITH	Huron Leonard	Lincoln and Welland Regiment, March 8, 1945, Ohsweken, Ontario.
Private	*SMITH	William George	Royal Hamilton Light Infantry, October 3, 1944, Ohsweken, Ontario.
Private	*SNAKE	Eli	Lincoln and Welland Regiment, January 28, 1945, Chippewas of the Thames, Muncey, Ontario.
Private	SNAKE-PERSON	Joseph	Royal Canadian Infantry Corps, April 4, 1942, Blackfoot Band, Gleichen, Alberta.
Private	SQUINAHAN	Francis Johnny	Canadian Scottish, September 20, 1946, Alkali Lake Band, Alkali Lake, British Columbia.
Trooper	*STINSON	Stanford Frederick	Sherbrooke Fusileers, July 8, 1944, Rama Band, Langford, Ontario.
Gunner	STINSON	Sidney Miles	Royal Canadian Artillery, March 20, 1942, Christian Island, Ontario.
Rifleman	*STOCK	Herman	Queen's Own Rifles of Canada, June 6, 1944, Gibson Band, Parry Sound, Ontario.
Trooper	*STONEFISH	Arnold	British Columbia Dragoons, June 8, 1944, Moravians of the Thames, Thamesville, Ontario.
Trooper	*STONEFISH	Lawrence	Lord Strathcona's Horse (Royal Canadians) September 23, 1944, Moravians of the Thames, Thamesville, Ontario.
Private	*SWANSON	George Bernard Alexander	Royal Hamilton Light Infantry, March 2, 1945, Chapleau, Ontario.
Private	*SWANSON	Stewart Henry	Lincoln and Welland Regiment, July 31, 1944, Chapleau, Ontario.
Gunner	*TAYLOR	George	Royal Canadian Artillery, January 17, 1945, Curve Lake Band, Curve Lake, Ontario.
Rifleman	*THOMAS	Donald	Regina Rifles, June 6, 1944, Peepeekisis Band, Lorlie, Saskatchewan.
Private	*THOMAS	Ernest	Canadian Scottish Regiment, July 8, 1944, Kamloops Band, Kamloops, British Columbia.

Private	*THOMAS	Herman Fletcher	Essex Scottish, July 30, 1944, Kettle Point Band, Forest, Ontario.
Private	THOMAS	James Oliver	Seaforth Highlanders of Canada, May 2, 1945, Peguis Band, Hodgson, Manitoba.
Corporal	*THOMAS	Peter Alex	Canadian Scottish Regiment, March 30, 1945, Stellaquo Band, Fraser Lake, British Columbia.
Lance Corporal	*THUNDER	Oliver Lawrence	Queen's Own Cameron Highlanders of Canada, July 22, 1944, Buffalo Point Band, Middleboro, Manitoba.
Private	*TOMMY	Francis	Royal Canadian Army Service Corps, March 22, 1944, Nanaimo Band, British Columbia.
Sergeant	*TOPPING	Charles Clinton	No. 226 (RAF) Squadron, August 26, 1941, Bay of Quinte, Marysville, Ontario.
Private	*TRUMBLEY	Walter Peter	North Shore Regiment, July 4, 1944, Tobique Reserve, Maliseet, New Brunswick.
Private	*TYEE	Philip	Calgary Highlanders, September 8, 1944, Pinchie Lake, British Columbia.
Private	*UNDER-WOOD	Edward	Canadian Scottish Regiment, November 17, 1945, Tsawout Band, Saanichton, British Columbia.
Private	VERANEAU	A. Albert	Royal Winnipeg Rifles, December 12, 1943, Rainy Lake Band, near Fort Frances, Ontario.
Private	*VERSAILLES	Peter	Loyal Edmonton Regiment, December 23, 1943, Grande Prairie, Alberta.
Private	*WABISCA	Emery	Loyal Edmonton Regiment, Big Prairie, Alberta, August 5, 1943.
Gunner	WADSWORTH	William Frederick	Royal Canadian Artillery, November 7, 1945, Blood Reserve, Cardston, Alberta.
Guardsman	*WAKEGIJIG	Clarence Wilfred	Canadian Grenadier Guards, February 2, 1945, Manitoulin Island, Cutler and Krugerdorf, Ontario.
Rifleman	*WALKER	Norman Stanley	Regina Rifles, July 8, 1944, Okanese Band, Balcarres, Saskatchewan.
Rifleman	*WELBURN	Francis William	Royal Winnipeg Rifles, April 20, 1945, Winnipegosis, Manitoba.
Gunner	WEMIGWANS	Felix	Royal Canadian Artillery, May 7, 1945, Manitowaning, Manitoulin Island, Ontario.
Private	*WHITFORD	David	South Saskatchewan Regiment, July 23, 1944, Sweetgrass Band, Prongua, Saskatchewan.
Private	*WILLIAMS	Harley James	Essex Scottish, March 8, 1945, Sarnia Band, Sarnia, Ontario.
Private	WILLIAMS	Isadore Gabriel	Royal Canadian Army Service Corps,

			March 13, 1947, St. Mary's Band, Cranbrook, British Columbia.
Private	*WILLIAMS	Roy Henry	Royal Hamilton Light Infantry, August 12, 1944, Ohsweken, Ontario.
Rifleman	*WILLIAMS	Walter J.J.	Regina Rifles, August 19, 1944, Tsawwassen Band, Delta, British Columbia.
Private	*WOOD	Clifford	Seaforth Highlanders of Canada, May 31, 1944, Saddle Lake, Alberta.
Gunner	*WRIGHT	Edwin	Royal Canadian Artillery, July 11, 1944, Walpole Island Band, Wallaceburg, Ontario.
Private	*YELLOWFLY	Gordon	Seaforth Highlanders of Canada, December 27, 1943, Blackfoot Reserve, Gleichen, Alberta.
Private	*ZACHARIAH	Willard	Hastings and Prince Edward Regiment, November 3, 1943, Desoronto, Ontario.

APPENDIX E

Honours and Awards

Second World War, 1939-1945

				Award
Pilot Officer	BOLDUC	Willard John	No.15 (RAF) Squadron, Ontario.	DFC
Private	BRANT	Huron Eldon	Hastings and Prince Edward Regiment, Ontario.	MM
Sergeant	BYCE	Charles Henry	Lake Superior Regiment, Ontario.	DCM, MM
Sergeant	CAMPION	George Alexander	Loyal Edmonton Regiment, Alberta.	MM
Private	LAVALLEE	Michael Martin	Hastings and Prince Edward Regiment, Ontario.	MM
Lieutenant	MOORE	Victor Alexander	Royal Canadian Engineers, Saskatchewan.	MC
Private	MUNROE	George Thomas	Queen's Own Cameron Highlanders of Canada, Saskatchewan.	MM
Rifleman	NAHWEGE ZHIC	Charles	Queen's Own Rifles of Canada, Ontario.	MM
Gunner	PATRICK	Dick	Royal Canadian Artillery, British Columbia.	MM
Corporal	PATTERSON	Welby Lloyd	Argyll and Sutherland Highlanders of Canada, Ontario.	MM
Sergeant	PRINCE	Thomas George	First Special Service Force, Manitoba.	MM U.S. Silver Star
Corporal	SPENCE	John Robert	12th Manitoba Dragoons (18th Armoured Car Regiment), Manitoba.	MM
Private	WEBSTER	Frederick	Seaforth Highlanders of Canada, British Columbia.	MM

Honours and Awards, Second World War

British Empire Medal (Civil)

"For excellent leadership, loyalty to the British Crown and fine example shown to the Indians throughout Canada":

CRATE,   Chief Andrew,
            Norway House Band,
            Norway House, Manitoba.

GAMBLE,   Chief Edward,
            Kitkatla Band,
            Kitkatla, British Columbia.

MOSES,   Chief Peter,
            Old Crow Band,
            Old Crow, Yukon Territory.

WINDIGO,   Chief Charlie,
            Nicickousemenecaning Band,
            Fort Frances, Ontario.

APPENDIX F

Indian land sold to Soldier Settlement Board.

Saskatchewan

Mistawasis	No	103	15,900.	acres	$ 198,576.
Ochapowace	No	71	18,223.4	acres	$ 164,160.
Muskeg Lake	No	102	8,083.3	acres	$ 135,000.
Poor Man	No	88	8,075.	acres	$ 92,920.
Piapot	No	75	16,318.	acres	$ 208,640.
Kahkewistahaw	No	72	1,903.56	acres	$ 28,652.
Cowessess	No	73	320.	acres	$ 3,200.
Big River	No	118A	980.	acres	$ 16,600.
	Total		69,803.26	acres	$ 831,148.

Alberta

Saddle Lake	No	125	8,960.	acres	$ 89,600.
Bobtail	No	139	6,926.79	acres	$ 79,862.
	Total		15,886.79	acres	$ 169,462.

British Columbia

Sumas	No	7	153.5	acres	$ 12,280.
	Grand Total		84,843.55	acres	$1,012,890.
Fort St. John	No	172	7,924.3	acres	$ 70,000. (Second World War)

(sold to the Director - Veterans' Land Act in 1948)

1. Letter, F.J. Singleton, Director,
Lands, Indian and Northern Affairs Canada,
July 21, 1982, to Fred Gaffen.

ABBREVIATIONS

AAG	Assistant Adjutant General		NCO	Non-commissioned officer
A/S Sgt	Acting Staff Sergeant		OBE	The Most Excellent Order of the British Empire
Bdr	Bombardier		OC	Officer Commanding
BEM	British Empire Medal		OC	Order of Canada
Bn	Battalion		PC	Privy Council
Cdr	Commander		PIAT	Projectile Infantry Anti-Tank
Col	Colonel		P/O	Pilot Officer
CO	Commanding Officer		POW	Prisoner of War
Cpl	Corporal		PPCLI	Princess Patricia's Canadian Light Infantry
CPO	Chief Petty Officer			
DCM	Distinguished Conduct Medal		Pte	Private
F/O	Flying Officer		RAF	Royal Air Force
FS	Flight Sergeant		RCAF	Royal Canadian Air Force
Gnr	Gunner		Rfn	Rifleman
HE	High Explosive		RHLI	Royal Hamilton Light Infantry
LAC	Leading Aircraftman		RSC	Revised Statutes of Canada
L/Sgt	Lance Sergeant		Sgt	Sergeant
Lt	Lieutenant		Spr	Sapper
Lt Col	Lieutenant Colonel		SS	*Schutzstaffel* (Protective Unit)
Maj Gen	Major General		Tpr	Trooper
MC	Military Cross		WO2	Warrant Officer Second Class
MM	Military Medal			

ACKNOWLEDGEMENTS

Institutions

AUSTRALIAN WAR MEMORIAL

CANADIAN ETHNOLOGY SERVICE, NATIONAL
MUSEUM OF MAN, NATIONAL MUSEUMS OF
CANADA
   Dr. T.J. C. Brasser
   Dr. G.M. Day
   Dr. M.K. Foster
   Dr. J.G. Taylor

CANADIAN WAR MUSEUM
   L.F. Murray

COMMONWEALTH WAR GRAVES COMMIS-
SION, CANADIAN AGENCY
   Pat Grieve
   June Buck
   Paulette Popowick
   Mike Newell

DEPARTMENT OF INDIAN AND NORTHERN
AFFAIRS, CANADA
   Treaties and Historical Research:
   John Leslie and staff

   Lands Branch:
   Kate Fawkes
   F.J. Singleton

   Library:
   Jean McNiven

DEPARTMENT OF INTERNAL AFFAIRS,
HISTORICAL BRANCH, NEW ZEALAND

DEPARTMENT OF VETERANS AFFAIRS,
AUSTRALIA

DIRECTORATE OF HISTORY, NATIONAL
DEFENCE HEADQUARTERS, CANADA
   Paul Marshall
   Dave Kealy

E & K PRODUCTIONS (PHOTOGRAPHY)
   Karel Valenta

GLENBOW ARCHIVES

NATIONAL LIBRARY OF CANADA

PUBLIC ARCHIVES OF CANADA
   Manuscript Section - Indian and Nor-
   thern Affairs:
   Dave Hume
   Bob Armstrong
   Bill Russell

   National Personnel Records Centre

ROYAL CANADIAN LEGION

STATISTICS CANADA

U.S. DEPARTMENT OF THE ARMY, CENTER OF
MILITARY HISTORY

U.S. DEPARTMENT OF THE INTERIOR, BUREAU
OF INDIAN AFFAIRS

Individuals

John Griffin, Ottawa
Ken Macpherson, Toronto
Allan Quandt, La Ronge, Saskatchewan
Carl Vincent, Stittsville, Ontario

BIBLIOGRAPHY

Primary Sources

My main source of written information about Indians in the First and Second World Wars is the Records of the Department of Indian Affairs, located in the Public Archives of Canada, Ottawa, RG 10, Volume 6762 to 6806. Soldier Settlement of Indian Soldiers after the First World War can be found in RG 10, 7484-7536. War diaries of the First and Second World Wars are also held by the Public Archives of Canada. The National Personnel Records Centre has service records of individuals. Additional files relating to Indian land purchased by the Soldier Settlement Board and the Veterans Land Administration are to be found in the files of the Department of Indian Affairs and of the Department of Veterans Affairs.

Annual Reports of the Department of Indian Affairs, 1914-1920.
Ottawa, King's Printer, 1915-1921.

Annual Reports of the Department of Mines and Resources, Indian Affairs Branch, 1939-47.
Ottawa: King's Printer, 1940-48.

The Indian Missionary Record, 1939-1945.
Archives, Oblate Fathers, Ottawa.

Land Settlement; Reports of the Soldier Settlement Board of Canada, 11 Vols.
Ottawa: King's Printer, 1921-37.

Secondary Sources

Books

Adams, Howard.	*Prison of Grass: Canada from the Native Point of View.* Trent Native Series, No. 1. Toronto: New Press, 1975.
Anderson, D.R. and A.M.	*The Metis People of Canada: A History.* Toronto: Gage, 1978.
Anonymous.	*Book of Remembrance, 1914-1918.* [Department of Veterans Affairs].
Anonymous.	*Book of Remembrance, 1939-1945.* [Department of Veterans Affairs].
Berton, Pierre.	*The Promised Land: Settling the West, 1896-1914.* Toronto: McClelland and Stewart Ltd., 1984.
Cooke, O.A.	*The Canadian Military Experience, 1867-1967: A Bibliography.* Ottawa: Department of Supply and Services, 1979.
Cowan, James.	*The Maoris in the Great War.* Wellington: Whitcombe and Tombs, 1926.
Dickson, Lovat.	*Wilderness Man: The Strange Story of Grey Owl.* Toronto: Macmillan, 1973.
Dobbin, G.M.	*The One-and-a-Half Men: The Story of Jim Brady and Malcolm Norris, Metis Patriots of the Twentieth Century.* Vancouver: New Star Books, 1981.

Dowe, Francís S.

The Canadian Military Register of Foreign Awards. Ottawa: privately printed, 1979.

England, Robert.

Discharged: A Commentary on Civil Re-establishment of Veterans in Canada. Toronto: Macmillan, 1964.

Gordon, Harry.

The Embarrassing Australian: The Story of an Aboriginal Warrior. London: Angus and Robertson, 1963.

Haycock, R.G.

The Image of the Indian: The Canadian Indian as a subject and concept in a sampling of popular national magazines read in Canada, 1900-1970. Waterloo: Waterloo Lutheran University, 1971.

Jackson, Louis.

Our Caughnawagas in Egypt: A Narrative of What Was Seen and Accomplished by the Contingent of North American Indian Voyageurs Who Led the British Boat Expedition for the Relief of Khartoum up the Cataracts of the Nile. Montreal: W.M. Drysdale, 1885.

Kidd, Bruce.

Tom Longboat, Don Mills, Ontario: Fitzhenry and Whiteside, 1980.

Knight, Rolf.

Indians at Work: An Informal History of Native Indian Labour in British Columbia, 1858-1939. Vancouver: New Star Books, 1978.

Lussier, A.S. and D.B. Sealey, Editors.

The Other Natives: The-les Metis. Vols 1-3. Winnipeg: Manitoba Metis Federation Press and Editions Bois-Brules, 1978-80.

MacEwan, J.W. Grant.

Fifty Mighty Men. Saskatoon: Modern Press, 1958.

MacEwan, J.W. Grant.

Portraits from the Plains. Toronto: McGraw-Hill, 1971.

McBride, Herbert W.

A Rifleman Went to War. Plantersville, South Carolina: T.G. Samworth Small Arms Technical Pub. Co., 1935.

Mountain-Horse, Mike.

My People the Bloods. Calgary: Glenbow-Alberta Institute and Blood Tribal Council, 1974.

Nicholson, G.W.L.

Canadian Expeditionary Force, 1914-1919. (Official History of the Canadian Army in the First World War). Ottawa: Queen's Printer, 1964.

Nicholson, G.W.L.

The Canadians in Italy, 1939-1945. (Official History of the Canadian Army in the Second World War, Volume II). Ottawa: Queen's Printer, 1956.

Patterson, E. Palmer II,

The Canadian Indian: A History Since 1500. Don Mills: Collier-Macmillan, 1972.

Patterson, Palmer and Nancy-Lou.

The Changing People: A History of the Canadian Indians. Don Mills: Collier-Macmillan, 1971.

Ponting, J. Rick and Robert Gibbons.

Out of Irrelevance. Calgary: privately printed, 1980.

Price, John A.

Indians of Canada: Cultural Dynamics. Scarborough, Ontario: Prentice-Hall, 1979.

Price, A. Grenfell.

White Settlers and Native Peoples: An Historical Study of Racial Contacts between English-speaking Whites and Aboriginal Peoples in the United States, Canada, Australia and New Zealand. Melbourne, Australia: Georgian House, 1950.

Sanders, Helen, ed.

Album of Honor for Brant County, World War II, 1939-1945. Brantford: Kinsmen Club, 1946.

Sawchuk, Joe and Patricia, and Theresa Ferguson.

Metis Land Rights in Alberta: A Political History. Edmonton: Metis Association of Alberta, 1981.

Schull, Joseph.	*Veneration for Valour.* Ottawa: Information Canada, 1973.
Sealey, D.B., ed.	*Famous Manitoba Metis.* Winnipeg: Manitoba Metis Federation Press, 1974.
Sealey, D.B. and V.J. Kirkness, eds.	*Indians Without Tipis: A Resource Book by Indians and Metis.* Winnipeg: William Clare Ltd., 1973.
Sealey, D.B. and A.S. Lussier.	*The Metis: Canada's Forgotten People.* Winnipeg: Manitoba Metis Federation, 1975.
Sealey, D.B.	*Jerry Potts.* Don Mills, Ontario: Fitzhenry and Whiteside, 1980.
Sealey, D.B.	*Questions and Answers Concerning the Metis.* Winnipeg: Manitoba Metis Federation, 1973.
Sealey, D.B. and Peter Van de Vyvere.	*Thomas George Prince.* Manitobans in Profile, Winnipeg: Peguis Publishers, 1981.
Shimony, A.A.	*Conservatism Among the Iroquois at the Six Nations Reserve.* New Haven: Yale University Press, 1961.
Sluman, Norma and Jean Goodwill.	*John Tootoosis: Biography of a Cree Leader.* Ottawa: Golden Dog Press, 1982.
Smith, Donald B.	*Long Lance: The True Story of an Imposter.* Toronto: Macmillan, 1982.
Stacey, C.P.	*Arms, Men and Governments: The War Policies of Canada, 1939-1945.* Ottawa: Queen's Printer, 1970.
Stacey, C.P.	*Six Years of War: The Army in Canada, Britain and the Pacific.* (Official History of the Canadian Army in the Second World War, Volume I). Ottawa: Queen's Printer, 1955.
Stacey, C.P.	*The Victory Campaign: The Operations in North-West Europe, 1944-45.* (Official History of the Canadian Army in the Second World War, Volume III). Ottawa: Queen's Printer, 1960.
Stanley, George F.G.	*Canada's Soldiers, 1604-1954: The Military History of an Unmilitary People.* Toronto: Macmillan, 1954.
Wheeler, Victor W.	*The 50th Battalion in No Man's Land.* Calgary: Alberta Historical Resources Foundation, 1980.
Wilson, Barbara M. ed.	*Ontario and the First World War 1914-1918: A Collection of Documents.* Toronto: University of Toronto Press, 1977 (Champlain Society Publications, Ontario Series, 10).
Woods, Walter S.	*Rehabilitation (A Combined Operation): Being a History of the Development and Carrying Out of a Plan for the Re-establishment of a Million Young Veterans of World War II by the Department of Pensions and National Health.* Ottawa: Queen's Printer, 1953.

BIBLIOGRAPHY

Articles

Amy, Lacey.	"An Eskimo Patriot" (John Shiwak), *The Canadian Magazine,* Vol. LI, No. 3, July 1918, pp 212-218.
Ashton, E.J.	"Soldier Land Settlement in Canada", *The Quarterly Journal of Economics,* Vol. XXXIX, May 1925, pp 488-498.
Cuthand, Stan.	"The Native Peoples of the Prairie Provinces in the 1920's and 1930's",

pp 31-42, in *One Century Later, Western Canadian Reserve Indians Since Treaty 7.* Ed. by Ian A.L. Getty and Donald B. Smith. Vancouver: University of British Columbia, 1978.

Dempsey, James. "The Indians and World War One", *Alberta History,* Vol. XXXI, No. 3, Summer 1983, pp 1-8.

Fraser, Blair. "But the Red Men Didn't Vanish!" *Maclean's Magazine,* LXIII, June 1, 1950, pp 8-9, 52-55.

Godsell, Philip H. "Our First Indians Do Their Bit", *Dalhousie Review,* Vol. XXI, No. 3, October 1941, pp 287-292.

Holm, Tom. "Fighting a White Man's War: The Extent and Legacy of American Indian Participation in World War II", *Journal of Ethnic Studies,* (Summer 1981), pp 69-81.

Jenness, Diamond. "Canada's Indians Yesterday. What of Today?" *The Canadian Journal of Economics and Political Science,* Vol.20, No. I, (February 1954), pp 95-100.

MacInnes, T.R.L. "History of Indian Administration in Canada", *The Canadian Journal of Economics and Political Science,* Vol. 12, No. 3, August 1946, pp 387-394.

Paudash, A.R. "I Married an Indian", *Maclean's Magazine,* LIV, December 1, 1951, pp 26-28.

Porter, McKenzie. "Warrior" (Tommy Prince), *Maclean's Magazine,* September 1, 1952, pp 11, 49-52.

Raddall, Thomas H. "Sam Glode: Travels of a Micmac", *Cape Breton's Magazine,* No. 35, January 1984, pp 21-29.

Scott, Duncan Campbell. "The Canadian Indians and the Great World War", *Guarding the Channel Ports,* Vol. III of Canada in the Great World War, (Toronto 1919), pp 285-329.

Stanley, George F.G. "The Indian Background of Canadian History", *Canadian Historical Association Annual Report,* 1952, pp 14-21.

------ "The Indians in the War of 1812", *Canadian Historical Review,* Vol. XXXI, No. 2, June 1950, pp 145-165.

------ "The Significance of the Six Nations Participation in the War of 1812", *Ontario History,* Vol. LV, No. 4, December 1963, pp 215-231.

U.S. Department of the Interior, Office of Indian Affairs. "The American Indian in the World War", Bulletin 15, 1927. 4 p.

Wise, Jennings C. "The American Indian in the World War", n.d. unpublished. 28 pages (U.S. Army Military History Institute,Carlisle Barracks, Pennsylvania).

Reports

Thompson, A.T. *Royal Commission to Investigate and Inquire Generally into the Affairs of the Six Nations Indians.* Ottawa: King's Printer, 1924.

Fawkes, Kate. "The Veterans Land Act: Its Application with regard to Indian Veterans". Unpublished research paper. Ottawa: Department of Indian Affairs and Northern Development, 1980, pp 1-19 and appendices.

RES Policy Research Inc.   "Indian Veterans and Veterans' Benefits in New Brunswick and Prince Edward Island", National Indian Veterans' Association, 1984.

Native Law Centre, University of Saskatchewan. *Indian Veterans Rights* (Report No. 3), 1979.

Sweeny, Alastair. "Government Policy and Saskatchewan Indian Veterans", Saskatchewan Indian Veterans Association, 1979.

Taylor, John Leonard. *Canadian Indian Policy during the Inter-War Years, 1918-1931,* Ottawa: Department of Indian Affairs and Northern Development, 1984.

Income tax: 33
Influenza epidemic, 1918: 33,57
Inuit: 11,28,29,33,78
Indian Affairs, Dept of: 20,23,36,37,38,71

Indian Bands:
        Alderville, Ont: 17,28,50
        Bird Tail, Sioux, Man: 40
        Blackfoot, Alta: 39,68
        Blood, Alta: 30,39
        Bloodvein, Man: 10
        Brokenhead, Man: 49,55
        Cat Lake, Ont: 21
        Caughnawaga, Que: 16,23,25,67,72
        Chippewas of Nawash (Cape
          Croker) Ont: 53
        Cote, Sask: 40
        Curve Lake, Ont: 21
        Edmundston, NB: 21
        Eel River, NB: 70
        Fort Alexander, Man: 40
        Fort William, Ont: 16
        Golden Lake, Ont: 52
        Gull Bay, Ont: 30
        Hiawatha, Ont: 20,71
        Iroquois of St. Regis,
        Ont/Que: 23,31,72
        John Smith, Sask: 47
        Lennox Is, PEI: 21
        Long Lake, Ont: 17
        Metlakatla, BC: 22
        Mohawks of the Bay of Quinte,
          (Tyendinaga), Ont: 17,40,41,65,73
        Montagnais of Lake St-Jean,
        Que: 20
        Muscowpetung, Sask: 41
        Nipissing, Ont: 41
        Ochapowace, Sask: 35
        Oka, Que: 20,31
        Old Crow, Yukon: 69
        Parry Island, Ont: 28
        Peepeekisis, Sask: 47
        Peigan, Alta: 39
        Piapot, Sask: 41
        Port Simpson, BC: 19
        Red Pheasant, Sask: 26,40
        Shawanaga, Ont: 28
        Sheguiandah, Ont: 51
        Six Nations of the Grand River
          (Oshweken),
          Ont: 18,20,23,24,25,27,31,38,41,
          49,50,52,64,72
        Sydney (Membertou), NS: 21
        The Pas, Man: 21,37

Tobique, NB: 21
Wabigoon, Ont: 43
Walpole Island, Ont: 72
Waywayseecappo, Man: 22
Wikwemikong, Ont: 37

Jamieson, A/Cpl Harold: 52
Jamieson, CPO George Edward: 64
Jeffries, WO2 Samuel: 65
Jeremy, Cpl Charles: 44
Johnson, Pte William: 21

Keeper, Cpl Benjamin Joseph, MM: 26,27
Kejick, Ont: 18
Kenora, Ont: 43
King, Pte Maxwell Jacob: 41
King, Pte Nick 21,22,29
King, The Rt Hon William Lyon Mackenzie: 67,69
Kisek, Pte David, DCM: 18,19

LaBillois, Margaret (nee Pictou): 69,70
Labrador: 11,28,29,40,68
Lamirande, Pte Louis: 41
Last Post Fund: 38
Lathlin, Pte Richard: 37
Lavalee, Pte Ernest: 40
Lavallee, Pte Michael Martin: 52,53
Lemieux, Bdr J.A.: 59
Letendre, Pte Norman Joseph: 52
Littlecrow, Spr Harold Charles: 47-49
Loft, Lt Frederick Ogilvie: 72
Longboat, Pte Tom: 27
Long Lance, A/Staff Sgt S.C.: 26

MacAuley, Norman H.: 40
McDonald, Lt Hugh John, MM: 24,25
McDonald, Pte Philip: 28
MacDougall, Spr Donald Charles: 47-49
McLean, Pte George, DCM: 22
Macleod, Alta: 29,30
McLeod, Pte Alfred Joseph: 53
McLeod, Pte Charles David: 53
McLeod, Tpr John Joseph: 53
McLeod, John M.: 53
McLeod, Pte Malcolm John: 53
McLeod, Mrs Mary: 53
McLeod, Pte Max: 53
McLeod, Pte Reginald: 53
Manitoulin Is, Ont: 27,31,37,38,51,52
Maoris: 74,75
Maracle, Pte Francis: 40
Martin, L/Sgt Franklyn: 41
Martin, Pte Henry: 40
Martin, Oliver Milton: 24
Merritt, William Hamilton (1885-1918): 20
Metallic, Pte Patrick: 40

Methot, Pte Frank: 40
Michel, Pte Paul: 30
Middleton, Canon Samuel H.: 29,30
Military Service Act: 31
Millik, Pte Abia: 29
Misinishkotewe, Pte Francis: 27,37
Montgomery, Lt Jack: 76,78
Monture, Gilbert Clarence, OBE, OC: 25
Moore, Pte Bertrand Cyril: 40
Moore, Able Seaman Lloyd George: 45
Moore, Lt Victor Alexander, MC: 44
Morrisseau, Pte Edward Joseph: 40
Moraviantown, Ont: 28
Moses, Lt James David: 25
Moses, Chief Peter: 68,69
Mountain Horse, Pte Albert: 29
Mountain Horse, Pte Joe: 29
Mountain Horse, Pte Mike: 29
Munroe, Pte George Thomas, MM: 47

Nahwegezhic, Rfn Charles, MM: 51,52
Nahwegezhic, Pte Roland: 52
National Resources Mobilization Act: 66,67
Navajos: 47,77,78
Newnham, Bishop J.A.: 35
Ngarimu, Second Lieutenant, VC: 75
Noel, Pte Max: 40
Norris, Arnold William: 73
Norris, Malcolm: 73
Norris, Pte Russell John: 73
Northwest Territories: 11,22,28,68,69
Norwest, Pte Henry, MM and Bar: 27

Obey, Pte George: 41
Ortona: 43,44

Passchendaele: 17,18,21,24,25,26,28
Patterson, Cpl Welby Lloyd, MM: 50,51,52
Paudash, FS Elmer Robert: 70,71
Paudash, Sr, Pte George: 71
Paudash, Jr, Sgt George Reginald: 70,71
Paudash, L/Cpl Johnson: 20,71
Paul, Charles: 72
Pearson, Pte Daniel, MM: 22
Pegahmagabow, Cpl Francis, MM and two
    Bars: 28,37
Pensions: 36,37
Peters, Omer: 72
Plante, Marguerite Marie (nee St. Germain): 69
Power, The Hon Charles Gavan: 37
Prince, Sgt Thomas George, MM, Silver
    Star: 55,56,57

Rhineland, battle: 51
Riel, Louis: 11,28
Riel, Pte Patrick: 28

Roussin, Pte Joseph, MM: 20
Royal Canadian Air Force: 65,66,69,70,72,73
Royal Canadian Navy: 66

St. Germain, Sgt Joseph Flavien: 44
St. Paul, Alta: 57
Saimat, Pte John: 29
Salisbury Plain: 16
Sanderson, Pte Isaac: 40
Saunders, Pte Freeman: 29
Saunders, Lt Reg: 74
Scheldt, battle: 50
Scott, Duncan Campbell: 29,31,35
Semia, Pte William: 21,37
Sero, Pte Reuben: 18
Shingoose, Pte Frank Douglas: 41
Shiwak, L/Cpl John: 28,29
Siegfried Line: 51
Silverheels, Jay (Harry Smith):26
Sioux, Pte Jean Joseph Anthony: 40
Smith, Pte E.A. 'Smokey', VC, CD: 8,43
Soldier Settlement: 35,36,71
Somme: 17,25,31
Spence, Cpl John Robert: 49,50
Splicer, Pte Angus: 16
Stanley, Col The Hon G.F.G.(Lt-Gov of New
    Brunswick): 79,80
Stacey, Lt John Randolph: 25
Statute of Westminster: 33
Stodgell, Pte Roy: 40
Stone, Col James Riley, DSO and Bar, MC: 44,79
Stonefish, Pte George: 28

Teillet, Roger: 73
Tenant, Lt Col Mark: 39
Thomas, Rfn Donald: 47
Tinker, Maj Gen Clarence Leonard: 76
Tobico, Pte Robert: 17
Topping, Sgt Charles Clinton: 65

V-1 'flying bombs': 50
Valcartier, Que: 10,16,28
Versailles, Pte Peter: 44
Veterans' Land Act: 72
Vimy Ridge: 16,17,22,26,27
Vocational Training: 36

War Veterans' Allowance Act: 37
Webster, Pte Frederick, MM: 43
White, LAC Douglas: 40
Williams, Pte Enos, MM: 18
Winters, Pte William: 29

Ypres: 15,16
Yukon: 24,31,68,69

Infantry, First World War
        Princess Patricia's Canadian Light
            Infantry: 16,17,39,43,57
        Royal Newfoundland Regiment: 29
        1st Battalion: 21,28
        8th Battalion: 28,30
        20th Battalion: 25
        22nd Battalion: 20
        26th Battalion: 21
        49th Battalion: 24
        50th Battalion: 29
        52nd Battalion: 16,17,20,21,32
        90th Battalion: 28
        107th Battalion: 20,23,24,27
        114th Battalion: 20,23,24,25
        180th Battalion: 27
        249th Battalion: 10

Infantry, Second World War
        Alaska Territorial Guard: 78
        Alaska Scouts: 78
        Algonquin Regiment: 66
        Argyll and Sutherland Highlanders of
            Canada: 50,51
        Black Watch (Royal Highland Regiment) of
            Canada: 49
        Calgary Highlanders: 39
        Edmonton Regiment (see Loyal Edmonton-
            Regiment)
        Hastings and Prince Edward Regiment: 39,41,52
        Highland Light Infantry: 58
        Lake Superior Regiment (Motor):   53,54
        Lincoln and Welland Regiment: 51
        Loyal Edmonton Regiment: 43,44,52
        Pacific Coast Militia Rangers: 68
        Princess Patricia's Canadian Light
            Infantry: 16,17,39,43
        Queen's Own Cameron Highlanders of
            Canada: 47
        Queen's Own Rifles of Canada: 50,51,52
        Regina Rifles: 39,47,58
        Rocky Mountain Rangers: 68
        Royal Hamilton Light Infantry: 39,41
        Royal Rifles of Canada: 40
        Royal Winnipeg Rifles: 39
        Seaforth Highlanders of Canada: 43
        South Saskatchewan Regiment: 39,41
        Special Service Force, 1st: 55,56
        Winnipeg Grenadiers: 40

NAVY

Ships:

Athabaskan, HMCS: 66
Fort Brunswick, SS: 57
Haida, HMCS: 66
Huron, HMCS: 66
Olympic, HMT: 10,21
Iroquois, HMCS: 66
Johnston, USS: 76
Micmac, HMCS: 66
Nootka, HMCS: 66
St. Croix, HMCS: 45
Yorktown, USS: 76